DEDICATION

This book is respectfully dedicated to Charles John Huffam Dickens, Lionel Herbert Blythe (Barrymore), and Quincy Magoo, who taught me to love the Carol; *to my paternal grandmother, Caroline Rothbart Wichman, who taught me to love all such wondrous tales; and to my mother, DiAnn Kemper Wichman, who more than anyone else, taught me to love the ever-given gift that is Christmas.*

Lionel Barrymore as Ebenezer Scrooge. (CBS photo.)

STANDING *in the* SPIRIT *at* YOUR ELBOW

A History of Dickens' *Christmas Carol* as Radio/Audio Drama

by CRAIG WICHMAN

STANDING IN THE SPIRIT AT YOUR ELBOW
A HISTORY OF DICKENS' *CHRISTMAS CAROL* AS RADIO/AUDIO DRAMA
©2012 CRAIG WICHMAN

ALL RIGHTS RESERVED.

No part of this book may be reproduced in any form or by any means, electronic, mechanical, digital, photocopying, or recording, except for in the inclusion of a review, without permission in writing from the publisher.

Published in the USA by:

BEARMANOR MEDIA
P.O. BOX 71426
ALBANY, GEORGIA 31708
www.BearManorMedia.com

ISBN-10: 1-59393-220-0 (alk. paper)
ISBN-13: 978-1-59393-220-6 (alk. paper)

DESIGN AND LAYOUT: VALERIE THOMPSON

TABLE *of* CONTENTS

PREFACE . . . 1

ACKNOWLEDGEMENTS . . . 3

FORWORD BY FRED GUIDA . . . 5

INTRODUCTION . . . 7

STAVE 1: *THIS MUST BE UNDERSTOOD, OR NOTHING CAN COME OF THIS STORY*
HOW DICKENS' *GHOST STORY OF CHRISTMAS* CAME TO BE . . . 9

STAVE 2: *THE BEGINNING OF IT*
THE *CAROL* RANG OUT SOFTLY AT FIRST . . . 13

STAVE 3: *THE SCROOGE AWAKES*
TWENTY YEARS WITH LIONEL BARRYMORE . . . 31

STAVE 4: *THE REST OF THE SPIRITS*
THEY ALSO SERVE... . . . 79

STAVE 5: *COSTING BUT A FEW POUNDS OF YOUR MORTAL MONEY*
CAROLS OF NOTE ON RECORD . . . 93

STAVE 6: *CHRISTMAS PRESENT*
THE *CAROL* NEVER DIES! . . . 137

STAVE 7: *MAY THAT BE TRULY SAID OF US*
A *CAROL* CLOSE TO HOME . . . 149

APPENDIX: *MANY CALLS SCROOGE MADE THAT NIGHT*
A (YULE) LOG OF BROADCAST AND FOR HOME USE *CAROLS* . . . 161

BIBLIOGRAPHY/SOURCES . . . 201

INDEX . . . 205

AUTHOR'S BIO . . . 229

PREFACE

As we celebrate the 200th Anniversary of his birth, I can think of no better way to begin such a book than by paraphrasing the words of the true "Founder of this Feast," Charles Dickens:

I have endeavored in this little book to raise the ghostly history of some sounds, which shall not put my readers out of humor with themselves, with each other, with the season, or with me. May this haunt their houses pleasantly, and no one wish to lay it to rest.

Their faithful friend and servant,
C.W.
HOLIDAY SEASON, 2012

ACKNOWLEDGMENTS

My acting teacher Stella Adler once told us of a cousin who had just announced the publication of his new book to a friend. To the friend's amazed response the cousin replied, "No big deal—I just read eleven books, then wrote the twelfth!" There are a great many figurative "eleven books" for this author to thank. Chief among them:

Friends and fellow radio drama lovers including actor Arthur Anderson, founder of the "Friends of Old Time Radio" Jay Hickerson, writer William Nadel, and my Quicksilver Radio Theater family, who gave information, advice, and support.

Radio/audio devotees Travis Butler, Don Connelly, Ted Kneebone, Gary Theroux, Elizabeth McLeod, and especially a certain Anonymous Benefactor; Barrymore family biographer Margot Peters, and Mike McKinney of the Audio Book Company, for useful facts and recordings of programs.

Librarians John Shaw of the G. Robert Vincent Voice Library at Michigan State University, Jackie Willoughby of the New York Public Library Main Branch, Danielle Cordovez, Jeremy Megraw, Arlene Yu and the staff of the New York Public Library for the Performing Arts, Richard Holbrook of the Paley Center for Media (New York), Rebecca Cape and Cherry Dunham Williams of Indiana University's Lilly Library, and Ned Comstock of the USC Library, for invaluable help.

Steve Darnall of *Nostalgia Digest*, Jack French of *Radio Recall*, and Max Cheney of the *Lounge of The Drunken Severed Head* website, for previously hosting portions of the material in this book.

The Episcopal Actors' Guild, whose library furnished several rare research volumes, and in whose friendly ghost-filled garret, much of this work took shape; and the New Age Christmas Radio website, which whistled while I worked.

Neal Ellis, Andrew Fielding, and Ken Stockinger, whose estimable webcast *Radio Once More* has graciously hosted an annual *Carol* special by me for three years running.

Jill N. Johnston of Campbell Soup Company, and Todd M. Axelrod and Gaii Creed of History For Sale, for permission to reproduce precious illustrations.

Most especially, *Carol* company members and listeners through the years including Julie Ashton, Jane Blalock, Lonnie Burr, Richard Carlson, Tommy Cook, Michael C. Gwynne, Bob Grant, Jimmy Lydon, Shirley Mitchell, Bill Owen, Dick Van Patten, Simon "Stuffy" Singer, and Jay Stern, for their priceless memories.

Fellow *Carol* chronicler Fred Guida, for his kind introductory words.

And of course, the folks at BearManor Media: production manager Sandy Grabman, publisher Ben Ohmart, and designer Valerie Thompson, for their welcome and their help.

Last but certainly not least, my sister Camela Wichman Davis, who shared my first radio *Carol* with me, and my wife Bernadette Fiorella-Wichman, who has heard many *Carol*s with me now, and whose word processing made this draft acceptable to BearManor.

And over all, to crib a signoff from Johann Sebastian Bach—
SOLI DEO GLORIA.

FOREWORD

A few years ago I produced a book that attempted to document and discuss the seemingly endless parade of film and television adaptations of *A Christmas Carol*. And while I took great pains to make it as complete and accurate as possible, it didn't take me long to realize the enormity of my task. As a work of literature, the immortal *Carol* is surely in a class by itself—as is interest in adapting it for film, television and virtually every other medium imaginable.

However, in largely confining myself to film and television, my book just briefly touched on radio and recordings. As such, I knew that my task, while difficult, was highly manageable. Documenting radio and recorded versions of the *Carol* is quite another matter.

Many recordings have been reissued numerous times over the years in various formats. Finding all of them can be very difficult and in some cases it can be impossible to accurately pinpoint when a particular recording was produced and/or released. And as for radio, all I can say is that research into this particular medium makes film and television research look like the proverbial walk in the park; it is an area shrouded in mystery and misinformation for non-specialists.

For these reasons, and more, *Carol* fans and scholars are in Craig Wichman's debt for he has produced a book that has been sorely needed for as long as I can remember. However, as with my book, his is a work in progress. No one can find absolutely everything, new information will always be coming to light, and some questions may never be answered.

But take this book for what it is: A meticulously researched, well documented, and thoroughly enjoyable exploration of a critically important corner of *Carol* scholarship. In short, thanks once again to Mr. Wichman for producing what will undoubtedly prove to be a great read and an invaluable reference tool for many years to come.

—**Fred Guida**, author of *A Christmas Carol and Its Adaptations: Dickens's Story on Screen and Television* and the blog www.charles dickensonscreen.com.

INTRODUCTION

Picture if you will a brisk Christmas Eve of the early 1970s in the snowy countryside around Defiance, Ohio. A teenage boy and his young sister sneak away from the extended family festivities taking place in a wood-paneled basement, to hunker down on the carpeting in front of the hulking Entertainment Center upstairs. The strains of Bernard Herrmann conducting Tchaikovsky's *Theme from Piano Concerto No.1* (aka *Tonight We Love*) begin, and soon the two are whisked away to Queen Victoria's England—and somehow, to Franklin Roosevelt's America at the same time!

WOWO Ft. Wayne ("The 50,000 Watt Voice of Farming") was rebroadcasting Lionel Barrymore's classic 1939 *Campbell Playhouse* production of "A Christmas Carol"—furnished, most likely, by legendary radio syndicator Charlie Michelson. The show was as magical that night as when first heard on the eve of the Second World War, and its powerful dramatization of Dickens' heart-gripping tale of redemption was to be one of the main reasons why the present writer—only 4 years old when Classic Radio Drama was decimated by the American networks in 1962— became a life-long lover of "The Theater of the Imagination," as well as a sometime portrayer of Ebenezer Scrooge.

That brother and sister both still love that production to this day. Like your first children's book, your first song, or your first date, your first *Carol* is often one of those things that stays with you forever—as several other people we will hear from in these pages will attest.

Now, this specific radio production of THE classic Christmas Story (well, actually the second-most classic, though it *has* been nicknamed "The Fifth Gospel") by Orson Welles and the Mercury Theatre is a deserved legend. But is it the only one? Or one of only a few?

OH, no.

As we'll shortly see, the "audioization" of the *Carol* began a mere thirty-five years after its author's death and has continued unabated for over a hundred years, right up to the penning of these words in 2012.

(NOTE: There have been many books about the *Carol*, and many about the history of audio drama; but to my knowledge, this is the first one specifically about *Carol* audio drama. So though the information contained herein has been gathered and collated with as much care as the present author could muster over the course of several decades, no claim is made that this history is definitive. Corrections and additions are welcomed at the email address given at the back of the book.)

STAVE 1:
This must be Understood, or Nothing can come of this Story

"...I wept, and laughed, and wept again, and excited (myself) in a most extraordinary manner in the composition...of this little book..."
—*Charles Dickens, 1844*

Charles Dickens in 1842.
(Portrait by Francis Alexander.)

(Reader, your eyes do not deceive you, nor are your author's spelling skills so bad as to spell "chapter" s-t-a-v-e. That old word for the verse of a song was seen by Mr. Dickens as a fitting title for the sections of the little Christmas carol that he wrote, so we will offer him a tip of the Victorian topper with the same usage.)

In the summer of 1843, 31-year-old Charles Dickens was already a renowned writer. But his most recent work, *Martin Chuzzlewit*, was not generating money as quickly as he had hoped. And with four children, a wife who was expecting another, and an extended family that he helped to support, the fears about having enough money that he had borne since the sometime poverty of his childhood returned. While taking his daily walks among the common people on the "black streets of London," he decided to gift them with a holiday treat that would also quickly raise cash for himself. With little time left to create it, he would keep it short and use a preexisting foundation: the "The Goblins who Stole a Sexton" portion of his first novel, *The Pickwick Papers* (which just happens to be the story of a hard-hearted man who is shown the error of his ways by some otherworldly creatures.)

But as he began the partially business-oriented enterprise of his new "Ghost Story of Christmas," the concerns of his heart bore down on him again—but this time not the fear of having too little money, but of becoming someone who cared about having money too much! He later recalled about working on the piece that:

> "…Thinking whereof (I) walked about… fifteen and twenty miles, many a night when all the sober folks had gone to bed…(I became) so closely occupied with my little *Carol*…that I never left home before the owls went out, and led quite a solitary life.…"

(Night. It seems that the *Carol* has always been a creature of the night, touched by night's loneliness. By some strange mesmerism that the story still holds, this present study of it was written largely under the light of the moon, too.)

Work on the new novella *A Christmas Carol* was done by November—including the author's personal designing of it, with special binding and end papers, and hand-colored illustrations by John Leech.

And the First Edition of 6,000 was sold out by Christmas Eve.

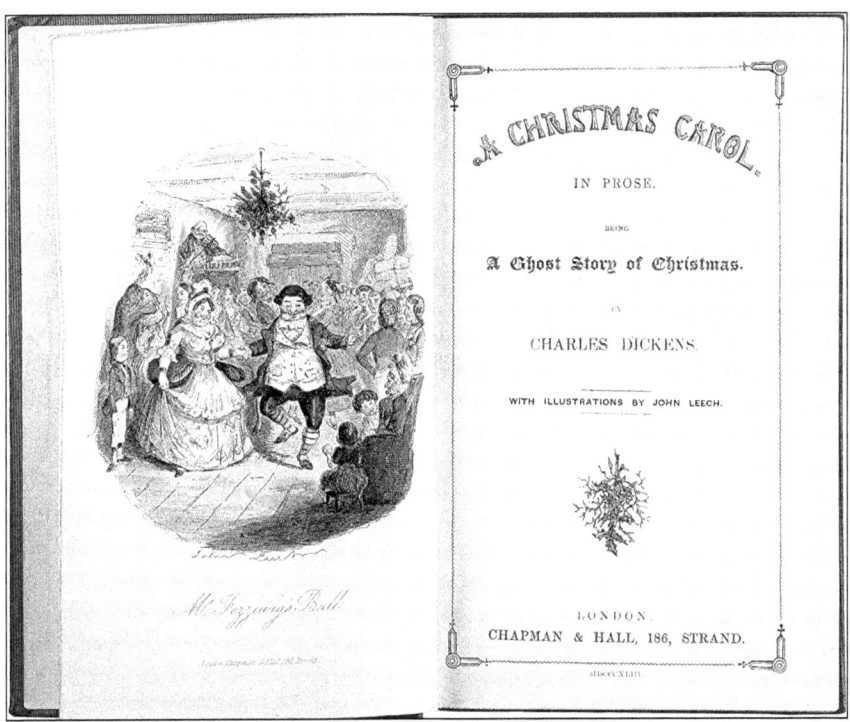

Charles Dickens' *A Christmas Carol* in its first public form.

Dickens had already written acclaimed works, and would create many more in the future; but this little fable, with its message of the cosmic destiny of every individual's everyday life, and of the surpassing power of personal redemption, struck a uniquely deep chord. Owners would later write to tell Dickens that they treasured their personal copy of the book by keeping it on its own special little shelf—and cogent to the topic of this present study, regularly read the story aloud to their families.

The new tale was an ever-expanding sensation. Almost immediately, the book was duplicated in unauthorized editions, and by mid-February of 1844, five unauthorized stage productions, such as *Scrooge, the Miser's Dream*, had already been mounted in London. By the following Christmas, the same practice had crossed the Atlantic to New York City as the *Carol*'s conquest of media beyond the printed page continued. And it was a very natural transition, as Dickens was an enthusiastic amateur actor himself; in fact, he was later a great success at his own public readings of his works, particularly this one. His plots are wonderfully dramatic, and his dialogue, richly human. The present author knows that firsthand, having dramatized his work (more on that, later) and never fails to be amazed when other adapters replace Dickens' golden fleece with their own chintz (more on that later, as well.)

Over the years, the *Carol* was pirated in an endless variety of printed formats, musicalized on stage, and at least as early as 1901, made into a silent film. That British *Scrooge, or, Marley's Ghost*, was directed by W.R. Booth; and an Edison studios faithful-for-its-short-length American movie from 1910 is still available on home video today.

Now, Dickens had always said that his story was best listened to in a darkened room. So when only a decade or so after the Silent Film productions, another new world-shaping medium was born, one that fit that manner of presentation to a "T," the *Carol* was there from the very start!

STAVE 2:
The Beginning of It

"What—what's that? Ah, the carol singers! ...Ah! The dear old Christmas bells!"
—Albert Whelan as Ebenezer Scrooge, circa 1905

Of course, the other medium that would affect the twentieth century as much as motion pictures was radio.

But the actual debut of Dickens' classic in the nascent "audio drama" field was not as a broadcast, but in a related format that developed in tandem with movies in the last decades of the 1800s—recorded sound.

Bransby Williams (born in 1870, the year Dickens died) was known as the "Hamlet of the Music Halls" in Great Britain. The actor/monologist was known for compact, one-man sketches that included imitations of famous theatrical figures of the time, as well as characters from Dickens. He had portrayed Ebenezer Scrooge on stage as early as 1896, and in 1905 he recorded for English Edison Records a cylinder entitled "Scrooge's Awakening." This was an abbreviated (but if like his later available recording of the piece, an energetic!) dramatization of the reformed miser's joyous Christmas Morning. Williams would go on to record various *Carol* excerpts in 1905, 1908, 1913, 1926, and 1933, and to play Scrooge in the character's first sound film portrayal (a 1928 short) and a 1950 BBC telecast; and several of his audio *Carol*ets have been reissued in changing formats up to the present day.

So his was the first Scrooge to blaze this new audio trail.

Or maybe not...

Sources vary as to date, but sometime between 1904 and 1906 (there is a documented *release* date of January, 1906), Australian-born entertainer Albert Whelan recorded a cylinder for Sterling Records in Great Britain variously known as "Scrooge's Christmas Morning" or "Scrooge's Awakening" (as the latter is the title actually

The first audio-recorded Scrooges, Albert Whelan and Bransby Williams, and their cylindrical media. (Courtesy of Austin Pickering; David Garratt, and Matthew Lloyd of www.arthurlloyd.co.uk; and Glenn Sage of

announced in the recording, perhaps they later renamed the released cylinder to differentiate it from Williams'?)

Whelan, too, was a star of the Music Hall circuit; a talented song-and-dance man and comedian, he would also appear in British films, and continue to record until shortly before his passing in 1961. At five years younger than Williams, he was only about 30 years old when he recorded his infectiously joyous performance as crotchety old Ebenezer. And the present author wonders if perhaps young Jim Backus' father didn't have one of these Whelan records around the house—because the grumbly, slightly sing-song voice that Whelan uses sounds a good bit like Mr. Magoo's in his animated *Carol* half a century down the road!

Though only a few minutes in length, the texts for these recordings are adapted from Dickens, they have supporting music and choruses, and "Turkey Boy" (hereafter, the title for the nameless lad who Scrooge deputizes on Christmas morn to buy the bird for the Cratchits' dinner) is also heard; so however brief, they do count as rudimentary audio drama. Considering the disputed date for the Whelan cylinder, until definitive confirmation arises we will grant Mssrs. Williams and Whelan a tie for "First Recorded Scrooge."

So in the first years of its second century, the *Carol* already was well poised to conquer yet another audio medium. And it would soon begin a march that would make it a solid holiday tradition on the radio, alongside such staples as Handel's *Messiah* and Irving Berlin's *White Christmas*. Right down to the present era, when broadcast radio drama is but a shade of what it was in its heyday, *Carol*s are aired at Yuletide.

So from here on, we'll touch on many of the radio and record productions down through the years for over a century now—as those two media even spawn offspring venues that grow to be well *Carol*ed themselves. (NOTE: From this point on, general information and editorial opinion about the various productions will usually be found in the front Essay section of this book, and greater detail as to venue, time, and personnel, in the back Log section.)

And we will pay special note to the work of an actor who became an institution in the story's lead role for two entire decades of that period, and whose presentation of the tale annually became for the United States what William Makepeace Thackeray had said that the book itself was for England: "a national benefit, and to every man or woman who (experiences) it a personal kindness."

In the interest of space, we will concern ourselves mainly with productions in America, the nation that many scholars credit with loving the story even more than does the land of its birth; the productions covered will be chiefly what are called "full-cast dramas," with a mention where appropriate of single-reader or small-cast versions; and this study will be more history than critique, not pausing for in-depth reviews of every production.

Now in the earliest days of civilian radio, entertainment programs consisted mainly of musical acts, speeches, or monologues by single performers, and occasional short sketches. But soon, performers and presenters realized that longer, fully-cast dramatic pieces could be presented in the medium. Often, local theater groups or traveling actors were the talent involved, and Dickens' masterpiece was an ideal choice for them: a strong story, beloved by the public—and in the fee-free public domain!

The first documented presentation of the *Carol* appears to have been on December 22, 1922, on pioneer station WEAF in New York. It was apparently of the simpler type of broadcast mentioned earlier, described as a 30-minute "reading" by Charles Mills, with music by violinist Grace McDermott and pianist Mary Burgum. Presentations over the following two years on stations WRC, WGY, WOAW, WOR, and the U.S.'s first commercially licensed station, Pittsburgh's KDKA, seem to have been similar in scope—perhaps even using Dickens' own trimmed-for-public-reading text, which was commonly used by readers then in non-broadcast presentations.

But on Christmas Eve of 1924, a leap forward took place that would probably have delighted the theater-loving author of the tale—Chicago's WMAQ Players performed "A Christmas Carol" on their *Play Night*. Though several earlier readings and recordings had evolved from simple reading into "impersonation" or "solo acting performance" territory, this appears to be the first full-cast dramatization of the tale ever broadcast.

Even at this early date, people were realizing that the medium of radio drama and a rich story like the *Carol* were a natural match. The Springfield, Massachusetts *Republican* reported that Charles Howard Mills' 1924's WEAF reading, "…received hundreds of appreciative letters coming from residents of 40 different states and many points in Canada and Bermuda." And the next year, a writer in the Portland *Oregonian* speaking about KGO Oakland's full-scale production noted with considerable foresight that:

Announcer Helen Hahn in the WEAF studio from which Charles Mills' historic first-ever broadcast *Carol* originated.

> "Radio listeners who are interested in drama over the air and its possible future developments can tune in…and hear a…work (that) has been especially adapted to sound…(with) music…which is intended to prepare the minds of the listeners for what is to follow, and create pleasant abstractions while the invisible scenery of time and space are being shifted…"

And to borrow an image from an author contemporary to Dickens, like Topsy this new practice "just growed":

> "NEVER BEFORE have radio broadcasters given such painstaking attention to preserving modern Christmas Eve custom and reviving that of the past. Some sort of Yuletide

program is offered by every station of prominence in the United States and Canada. Haendel's [sic] 'Messiah' and Dickens' 'Christmas Carol' continue to be well beloved, as is evidenced by many broadcasts tonight."

The same Christmas of that 1926 United Press syndicated radio listing, a "mini-network" hookup of WFBL, WGY, and WMAK broadcast a *Carol* by the Boar's Head Dramatic Society of Syracuse, N.Y. It may well have been announced by WFBL's announcer/station director Ernest Chappell, who was to have an illustrious radio career that included several later star-studded *Carols* with the likes of Orson Welles and RCA Victor.

And the following Christmas, the young National Broadcasting Company's Red group of stations (one of two early divisions, along with the Blue) aired the first true "network" *Carol*, another WEAF performance by Charles H. Mills, with violin music by Arcadie Birkenholz. (A musician of note who would later work with Arturo Toscanini, Birkenholz recalled in a conversation with radio historian William Nadel that he had been a part of the NBC network's gala debut broadcast on November 15, 1926.)

To be honest, Jacob Marley might have noted that these programs weren't *all* just hearty Christmas spirit—there was some Commerce involved! The *Oregonian* dutifully noted that KGW's 1928 offering was, "a Christmas token to radio folk bearing the good wishes of Charles F. Berg and his employes [sic]."

Another step into even fuller presentation was taken on Christmas Eve of 1928 when WOR out of New York, the first station to carry programming from William Paley's fledgling Columbia Broadcasting System, broadcast with 20 other stations a TWO-HOUR full-cast *Carol* with supporting musical score, followed by a program of choral caroling. (After having heard many productions of the story, the present author's opinion is that the most common 30-minute slot cannot do justice to the piece, while the occasional 60-minute length does the job well. 120 minutes would grant Dickens' textured plot real room to express itself—though at one sitting, it might tax the listening audience's perseverance a bit.)

The CBS broadcast was well received. The Decatur, Washington "Listening In" columnist wrote that:

> "...of all features of the evening, probably the best received was the Columbia chain's 'A Christmas Carol,' this is judging from the comments of fans heard Tuesday morning..."

But it had some worthy competition from Chicago that evening by way of early radio superstar Tony Wons. By this time, Menasha, Wisconsin's Anthony Snow had already performed the Bard's work over the airwaves, and he would soon become known nationally for his CBS *Scrapbook*, where he performed poetry from many writers, including his own listeners', in a warm, slightly purple style that especially endeared him to the fairer sex (in a way, he was a non-singing crooner.) And he evidently did Dickens proud, as "Listening in" continues:

> "...we failed to hear the Columbia interpretation of the story, but we did hear WLS' broadcast of it, and if the Columbia broadcast was any more interesting, it must have been perfect. Anthony Wand, [*sic*] poet, played the part of Scrooge, and played it perfectly. The ghost roles were impressively filled—but then every voice, every character, added to the interest of the presentation."

There was a regular bustle of *Carol*ing on the air in Chicago in 1928. This appears to be the first year that WGN aired a full-cast dramatization of the tale, following three annual readings by Scottish-born announcer Bill Hay (during the same era that he became *Amos 'n' Andy*'s first announcer, a position that he would hold for years.) And in 1926, six-year-old Shirley Bell had become the youngest member of the W-G-N Players—was she perhaps a part of this broadcast on the cusp of gaining her own national radio fame in 1929 as radio's *Little Orphan Annie*?

The record shows that in the early radio era, once a station or a network presented Dickens' tale it tended to return to it annually. "The CBS" as some called it then would *Carol* again regularly over the following Christmases by way of WABC, their New York City flagship station in those years. And we are blessed with information about their 1929 production by way of one of the first persons of color to work in American network radio.

Jamaican-born Vere Everette Johns was a veteran of the British service in WWI. In addition to his U.S. work in radio, he assisted early African-American filmmaker Oscar Micheaux. A newspaper writer as well, he eventually returned to Jamaica where he became an influential journalist and hosted a popular radio talent show.

Vere spread the word about his happy 1929 engagement to the folks back home in *The* (Jamaica) *Gleaner* of December 23rd:

> "LISTEN FOR VERE JOHNS CHRISTMAS EVE NIGHT
>
> A letter from Mr. Vere Johns came to hand on Saturday afternoon conveying the information that …he is now linked up with the Columbia Broadcasting System, Christmas Eve being his first appearance over station WABC (349 metres) and short wave station W2XE (49.18) …The feature in which he is taking part is a Dickens drama, but at the time of writing he did not know what character he would represent.
>
> Those of us who know his talents feel sure that whatever part is allotted to him he is going to do full justice to it. 'I would appreciate,' his letter says, 'your sending me a cable first, followed by a letter, and copies of the Gleaner containing reports from listeners so that I can inform the Columbia people.'
>
> …Johns is one of us—let us back him up!"

Jack Soanes, English actor and director, is to portray the role of Scrooge in a presentation of Dickens' Christmas Carol to be heard at 11 on Christmas Eve over the Columbia network. Try WADC, Akron.

1929 CBS *Carol* documenter and Christmas Past, Vere Johns, and newspaper publicity featuring his Scrooge, Jack Soanes. (Ad courtesy of an Anonymous Benefactor.)

The thrown gauntlet by Johns and *The Gleaner* was picked up. In the New Year's Eve 1930 edition, "S-W-4, Kingston" gave a report that is very evocative of early radio listening:

> **"FIRST REPORT ABOUT JOHNS BROADCAST**
>
> As requested, I report the result of my listening in to WABC on Xmas Eve; I use a 'Shortwave 4' and got sometimes two stations, WABC and W2XE at what I estimate to correspond

to about 49 and 25 meters on my dial. I listened to the 49 meter station.

I tuned in a few seconds after the synopsis narrator had begun, and with the exception of a sentence or two during my listening, was able to follow the performance on my loudspeaker. The volume was however by no means strong, and to get portions I had to be close to the speaker and listen attentively. The articulation of all the speakers was nevertheless very good. I experienced no static interruption…

I am not very familiar with Mr. Johns' voice, but felt I ought to recognise it. As the piece drew on I thought he was after all omitted, until I heard one of the spirits speak—the one that spoke as Scrooge, half awake, 'put his hand on the door.' This was shortly after 10.30 p.m., when the announcer said, 'May we interrupt the Dickens production to tell you that it is coming over the Columbia Broadcast system, WABC and W2XE.' The voice of the spirit in question had the deliberateness, clearness of pronunciation and tone of Johns. It sounded somewhat suppressed and solemn, to suit, I suppose, the role of the spirit. In a different role, this voice would, I think, have been heard to better advantage."

And in another letter to the same newspaper a week later, a detailed postpartum on this *Carol* is given by "The Ghost of Christmas Present" himself:

"VERE JOHNS, AND THE RECENT BROADCAST

Mr. Vere Johns, in a letter which is published below, tells us all about the 'Dickens' programme and the part he took in it:

'I have just received copies of the 'Gleaner' containing both your call to listeners and your comments after the broadcast was received and I am exceeding grateful to you for the prominence given. The magnificence of the production was impressive even to us in the studio: in one corner stood a huge Christmas tree elaborately decorated and lighted, to the right of that were the numerous effects, and near them the fourteen of us players with Mr. Don Clark and Miss Georgia Bacchus [*sic*] in charge; in front were Announcer and Narrator with four microphones while filling the rest of the studio were a large crowd of carol singers and a large orchestra under the conductorship of Mr. Howard Barlow.

For two hours we had been rehearsing while other studios were carrying on; then a call for dead silence at one minute to eleven, while all watched the uplifted hand of the control operator; down it came, and Dickens' 'Christmas Carol' was on the air over WABC and W2XE. Each player took the mike in turn, music and sound effects were appropriately interspersed under the watchful eyes and ears of respective directors, and the stroke of twelve saw the finish of what had been a co-ordinated performance carried through without a hitch.

Some glorious chimes were played and then our studio was switched off the air leaving us free to breathe and wish one another a merry Xmas. The critics although not particularising were unanimous in declaring that it was the best presentation of Dickens' famous story that they had ever heard....

I shall be glad to have reports not only as to my share of the broadcast but as regards to the entire reception with some detail as to how the thing came over—i.e. voices, music and effects, both yours and other listeners....

(As to the future) you can depend on it that whatever I do will be worthy of Jamaica and she shall enjoy equal notoriety with myself. I intend that the people of this country shall know of our island as she really is and not as they imagine that she is, and with voice, actions and pen I shall let them know her as far as they will permit me. Again thanking you for your courtesies and hoping to hear from you soon,

With best 1930 wishes,
VERE E. JOHNS.
New York.'"

We will hear even more detail about that new CBS studio in the heart of Manhattan's advertising district at 485 Madison Avenue soon.

Also there that Christmas Eve amongst the large cast that Johns describes were actor Jack Soanes as Scrooge, a role that publicity claimed he had "portrayed...many times on the London stage." Some sources mention him arriving in America from Canada around the time of this broadcast, and his career included Broadway roles such as general understudy in the original *Grand Hotel*, and an appearance in the Florida-produced movie, *Playthings of Desire*. Bob Cratchit was played by Allyn Joslyn, who appeared in literally thousands of radio broadcasts including the *Showboat* series, created the role of Mortimer Brewster in the stage debut of *Arsenic and Old Lace*, and later had a long career as a Hollywood TV and movie character actor that included the original *Heaven Can Wait*. And Tiny Tim was young Donald Hughes, who soon became a character part stalwart in the stock company of *Let's Pretend* with fellow *Carol*ers Dick Van Patten, Jimmy Lydon, and Arthur Anderson, who speaks of Donald in his book on the Nila Mack series:

> "'I liked acting,' Don once said, long after having retired. 'I like it to this day. I liked the companionship.' Don was also a much better actor than he would admit, to himself or anyone else. Jack Grimes would observe Don's performances, especially when he was playing a lead, such as Faithful John or Rumpelstiltskin, and claimed that you could see Don begin to do a truly brilliant piece of work, then suddenly seem to say, 'Oh, dammit—it's showing,' and pull back."

That comment shows the mark of an actor not only gifted, but self-aware. (As to his own work, we'll hear from Mr. Anderson again in the next chapter.)

The early Thirties were an era when as corporate entities are wont to do, the new radio networks were consolidating their power. One let its affiliated stations know that it would offer "the *exclusive* (italics mine) presentation, on the National Broadcasting Company networks…of Charles Dickens' immortal 'The [*sic*] Christmas Carol.'" And with that fiat several radio local Scrooges, veterans of early broadcast *Carol*s, probably found that they had received Bob Cratchit's threatened fate and "lost their situations." But never fear, for listeners were assured that on this 1930 NBC *Soconyland Sketches* series episode, "Arthur Allen will be heard in one of his masterpieces of radio characterization as 'Scrooge,' (and) Henry Fiske Carlton and William Ford Manley have made…one of their most careful and complete adaptations…."

The next year, NBC presented its *Carol* in another novel venue.

Their weekly journeys down London's Baker Street took a turn, as Richard Gordon put aside his usual guise of Sherlock Holmes to become Ebenezer Scrooge, and Leigh Lovell (Dr. Watson) told a tale adapted by series co-creator/writer Edith Meiser not from Doyle but Dickens. She, like many others, would visit the story again over time; in fact William Nadel, friend of the writer in her later years, says that the script she prepared at this time was the basis for several later *Carol*s of hers.

(Collector's Corner, 1931 edition: There is in circulation a recording of a forty-minute *Carol* that is sometimes identified as being produced by George P. Ludlam for NBC Syndication in 1931. From the presence of an actor's voice he recognizes, Willam Nadel dates it as from 1933–1934; and the present author agrees that the production style seems of that early era. But some sources maintain that it may in fact be from another production entity and/or an even later date—see the note later in this chapter concerning the December 25, 1937 Thesaurus broadcast. As to the contention some make that this program is actually the oldest extant BBC transcription, the fact that it sounds as if it has a largely American cast discounts that claim for this listener. If future research does confirm that this forty-minute production did indeed originate at NBC in 1931, it would almost certainly have been for off-net syndication; for the network had already presented its featured *Carol* on December 23 in the Holmes slot, and that was likely their "exclusive" one for that season, as had been 1930's *Soconyland* presentation.)

Meanwhile, CBS continued raising Dickens' Spirits too. Soanes and Hughes reprised their 1929 roles in 1930, and in 1931 Hughes' Tim would touch the heart of a Scrooge portrayed by seventy-year-old Robert Vivian (the character was often billed as "Old Scrooge" in this era.) Vivian was a London-born actor who had a thirty-year career on Broadway and in the silent and early sound cinema.

But there was perhaps a worrisome harbinger in the fact that the Hartford *Courant* said of 1930's CBS *Carol* that in the adaptation by Georgia Backus and Donald Clark (likely the same as their text for the 1929 Johns broadcast) "much of Dickens' original dialogue has been retained." That wording could imply that much also was *not* retained—and alas, when the rolling years brought the *Carol*

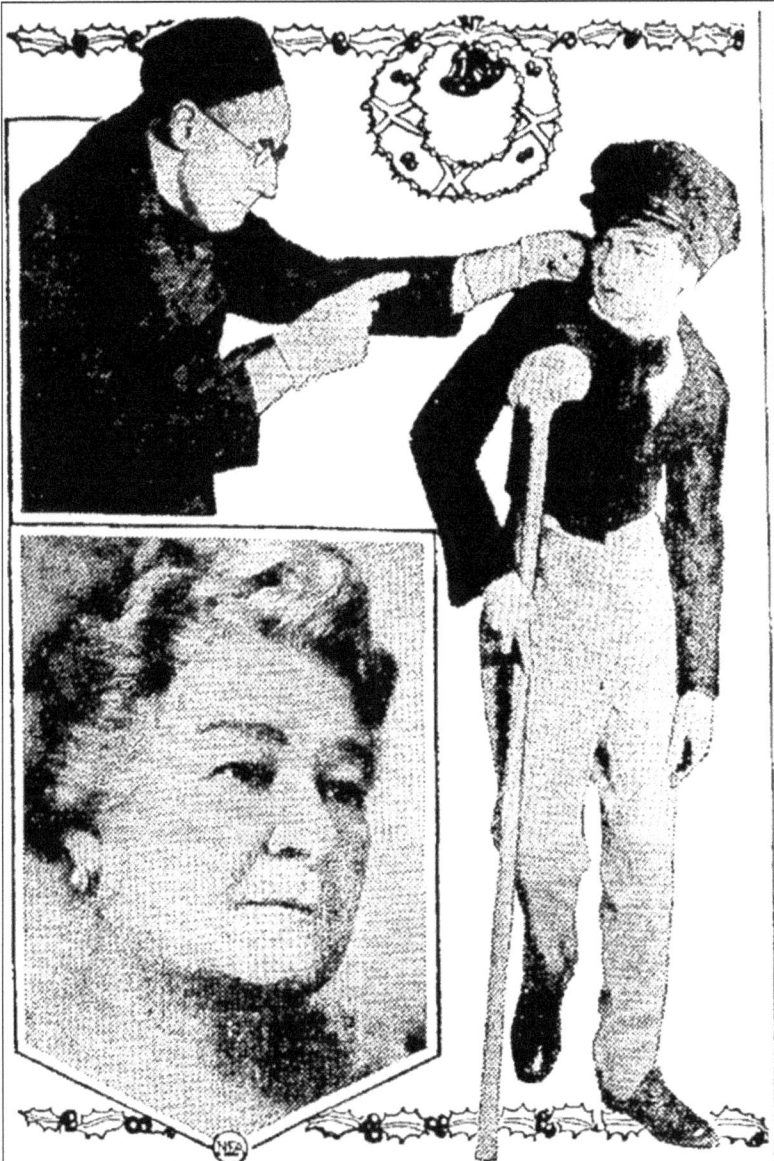

The Christmas spirit will be spread Christmas Eve by such examples as the annual presentation by CBS of Dickens' "Christmas Carol," with the same actors in the cast—Robert Vivian as "Scrooge" and Donald Hughes as "Tiny Tim," shown here and the singing of "Silent Night, Holy Night,' by Madame Schumann-Heink, inset, over an NBC network.

Newspaper announcement of Donald Hughes' return as Tiny Tim in 1931, with inset featuring another radio Christmas staple of the era. (Courtesy of an Anonymous Benefactor.)

around to the net again in 1933, not everyone in the audience at home was suitably enchanted by the script used:

> "To the Editor of the New York Times—A Listener's Criticism:
>
> Please, on behalf of the thousands of your readers who are lovers of Charles Dickens and his immortal 'Christmas Carol,' allow me space to protest the sacrilege that has just been practiced in broadcasting over WABC the garbled monstrosity of that beautiful story. Sacrilege! It is worse than that. Some license is permissible in adapting an author's work to dramatic form, but to deliberately change the theme, the purpose, the scenes and characters, and to put in the mouths of the latter atrocious expressions, even to the use of slang, is unbearable! The more so when it is recalled that the 'Christmas Carol' is, as Dickens wrote it, intensely dramatic in its opening, its climaxes and its ending, and needs no altering. Dickens knew what he was doing when he wrote it....
>
> Think of calling Bob Cratchit's 'goose' a duck over and over again. Every one knows or should know that 'there never was such a goose!' And, oh, mercy! Can you imagine Bob Cratchit saying to Tiny Tim at that wonderful Christmas dinner: 'There's oodles of gravy!' To think that any one [*sic*] could deliberately murder, quarter, and hang upon a gibbet that wonderful bit of home life, and Christmas dinner of the Cratchit family for millions of radio listeners.... Not one word can be cut from the cameo Dickens cut and wept over as he did so.

Marley's ghost does not go through the whole story as this version had it. The change was absolutely ridiculous. Some of the most beautiful lessons the story is meant to teach were lost. There was no need to introduce other characters than Dickens had provided. The attempt to rewrite Dickens's work as was done here calls for the severest condemnation from every Dickens lover.

—Harold F. Loekle
Allendale, N.J. Dec. 26, 1933"

Reader, pay heed to "St." Loekle's prophetic wisdom, which is almost equal to Jacob Marley's (who the present author agrees certainly has no place in the later story, after his very dramatic exit in the beginning!) We will have cause to think of "The Loekle Rule" much as we *Carol* on through the years and his thesis about the folly inherent in tampering with Dickens' original text is sadly proven right again and again.

But at least this 1933 production was narrated by famed Algonquin Round Table raconteur Alexander Woollcott (basis for the famous character *The Man Who Came To Dinner*), a life-long lover of Dickens. So maybe it wasn't *all* bad. And in any event, CBS would soon make amends.

For come the next Yuletide, their annual gift of the *Carol* would lay the cornerstone for what would become a radio—and Christmas—legend.

STAVE 3:
THE Scrooge Awakes

"...Present(ing)...the best-loved actor of our time, in the world's best-loved Christmas story..."

—*Orson Welles, 1939*

Christmas, 1934: the press trumpets the arrival of the actor who was to become the premier *Carol* standard-bearer of the radio era.

Lionel Barrymore will be heard over the air for the first time today, when he takes the part of the immortal "nasty man" in Dickens' "Christmas Carol."

On the afternoon of Christmas Day 1934, during that heady era of early national broadcasting (even *international*, considering that many radios then received shortwave, per the Jamaican response to the 1929 *Carol* just covered) CBS presented a "Variety Special" that originated from literally across the breadth of America. Newspaper ads humbly proclaimed it "THE WORLD'S GREATEST RADIO PROGRAM," and as it presented renowned M.C. Alexander Woollcott, Victor Young's orchestra, world-famous opera star Madame Schumann-Heink, "Funniest Woman in the World" Bea Lillie, George Olsen and His Music, Ethel Shutta, and the Apollo Club Chorus from Chicago, Don Cossack's Russian Male Chorus from New York, and a holiday drama with a Hollywood cast from Los Angeles, there was some truth to the adline.

And amidst all the program's bright offerings, the Washington Post "On The Air Today" columnist announced that:

> "…(the) reason (C.B.S.) has…to be excited over the big Christmas pageant at 2:30 this afternoon…is that Lionel Barrymore will be heard over the air for the first time ever when he takes the part of the immortal 'nasty man' in Dickens' 'Christmas Carol.'"

Yes, the diamond in this continent-spanning gold ring of a Christmas gift was actor Lionel Barrymore's debut performance of the role of Ebenezer Scrooge.

Born in 1878, Barrymore was descended from two famed American acting families, the Drews and the Barrymores. Bracketed by Ethel and John as middle child in a famed twentieth century performing triumvirate, Lionel is also the great uncle of today's Drew. He is perhaps best known today as Mr. Potter in another Christmas perennial, Frank Capra's film *It's A Wonderful Life*—a casting choice that owed much to his 1934 role here and what followed from it. Audiences back then had seen him on the Broadway stage since 1900, in parts including *Macbeth*; in silent film since D.W. Griffith's *Fighting Blood* of 1911; and as winner of the 1931 Best Actor Oscar for the Talkie *A Free Soul*. Lionel would be introduced by a fellow show business legend in a broadcast not long after this one as, "the best loved actor of our time," and for once, such words may not have been empty ballyhoo.

(Just for the record, the *New York Evening Post* referred to this

Undated, this photo appears to be the earliest character study of Lionel Barrymore as Ebenezer Scrooge; the one used in the newspaper piece at the beginning of this chapter was of the actor as Dan Peggoty from that 1935

Yuletide extravaganza as, "a special three-hour *commercial*," [italics mine], and just as surely as the cornucopia of performers and national scope of this production did not come cheap to its sponsor, we can trust that the Nash Motor Company made sure to remind listeners of their fine automobiles!)

A recording does not seem to be extant, but of the program's total three-hour length, the *Carol* may have lasted sixty minutes, as did CBS's in the year before it; or it may have been only thirty minutes, as that would be the length of the next season's. But whatever the duration of Mr. Ebenezer Scrooge's trials, Mr. Lionel Barrymore came out of them a bona-fide hit.

So come December 4, 1935, it was announced that not only would the star return to the role on the twenty-fifth of that year, but also that he had been signed to a new contract for an additional five years in the role. It was noted in the press that for a single annual event, this kind of long-term arrangement was unprecedented; but in fact, even that half-a-decade would be only the beginning of his time spent in Scrooge's drafty old house.

"Dickens' immortal 'Christmas Carol' has been read to children for many years and has been seen at Christmas pageants in tableaux and little stage plays. This year the youngsters over the country are going to have the treat of a lifetime."

Maybe the writer for the *New York American* had missed it, but of course those that had been of an age to listen already had the treat of Barrymore's Ebenezer the previous year. We don't know if then eight-year-old Buster Phelps had listened in 1934, but he did have the honor of taking part in the story next time around as Tiny Tim. Phelps' career began in 1931, and would include such films as *Little Men* and *Anna Karenina*, where he was the son of Greta Garbo and sometime Scrooge Basil Rathbone. He retired from films in 1949, and passed away in 1983.

The *American* writer went on to say that, "Lionel is fast becoming one of the greatest favorites on the air." And one at the New York *Herald Tribune* seconded the praise: "(his) characterization of Scrooge… will be an outstanding drama presentation over WABC Christmas Day…." To top it all off, *The Saturday Evening Post* carried a full page, full color ad for the broadcast with an evocative painting of Bob Cratchit with Tim on his shoulder by Norman Rockwell.

For their 1936 edition, CBS planned to do as NBC had a few seasons earlier, and present their *Carol* in the setting of an existing series—in this case, Friday's *Hollywood Hotel*, sponsored by Campbell's Soup, fell on Christmas Day that year. After only three years, a solid tradition was already being formed with this union of

As Lionel Barrymore began his engagement for six annual CBS *Carols* in 1935, a photo sitting in full costume and makeup produced a batch of publicity stills that would see use for years. The one used as Frontpiece of this book shows a pensive Scrooge; and here in the oddest of the set, Scrooge contemplates a truly *Tiny* Tim. (CBS photo.)

actor and story, and so the man himself was given generous column space in the papers to speak about his play to his public. (Such pieces are sometimes ghostwritten for celebrities; but as Lionel Barrymore was a creative, well-spoken man, both here and throughout we'll trust that the words attributed to him are indeed his.)

"'YE GHOSTS OF SCROOGE'
By Lionel Barrymore

One of the reasons why I enjoy playing the role of Scrooge in Dickens' 'Christmas Carol' each Christmas season over the Columbia network is the fact that I believe in ghosts.

Although Scrooge was confronted with three ghosts: namely, the ghost of Christmas Past—his memory; the ghost of Christmas Present—his intuition; and the ghost of Christmas Future—his imagination, people today may have as many as seven or eight ghosts haunting them. It all depends upon their experiences, for in the innermost recesses of every human mind there are the memories of the past, the intuitions of the present and the imagination of the future.

It is foolish to harbor awesome thoughts about ghosts for they are in reality man's conscience and therefore his best friend. If man refuses to accept them as such, they will force themselves upon him anyway as they did upon Scrooge when he had closed his eyes and heart to the spirit of Christmas season [sic] and the joy of living.

Happy Childhood Days.

It took the ghost of Christmas Present to remind Scrooge of his happy childhood days, and many are the Christmas days that I have been confronted with the ghost of my own childhood. I am always happy to know that my Christmases were no different from the millions of other children in the world. I see plainly the long awaited Christmas visit which Ethel, John and I made to Grandmother Drew's home in Philadelphia each year. I see father and mother returning on Christmas Eve from a long theatrical tour with their arms overflowing with tempting packages. There would be a fancy new dress or a china-faced doll for Ethel, a pair of boxing gloves or a shiny toy sword for John, and usually a new book or a paint box for me.

As the ghost of Christmas Past vanishes, I see the ghost of Christmas Present approaching. Although this same ghost showed Scrooge the homely simplicity of Bob Cratchit's Christmas Day and the quiet reverence for the One who had created the day, it shows me the American Christmas of today with its 11 o'clock risers who grab a hasty breakfast, rip open their gift packages, gasp out a thrilled 'Gee! Thanks! It's just what I wanted' and then rush out to a football game to cheer themselves further into the spirit of the day.

Nevertheless, despite the great change which has taken place between the Christmas of Scrooge's time and the Christmas of today, I sincerely believe there is still as much Christmas spirit as there was when Dickens wrote his immortal 'Carol' about Scrooge. I believe the whole world is still very much aware of the significance and tradition of Christmas, and that it is not so much how a person spends the day as it is how he feels in his heart.

Greedy Mode of Living.

> Although the ghost of Christmas Future showed Scrooge how tragic his future would be if he continued in his selfish, greedy mode of living, this same ghost is revealing to me now the eagerness with which America is waiting to hear the story of Scrooge's enlightenment again this year. The ghost shows me the thousands of letters which will again be sent from all over America confirming their love for this immortal Dickens' story and their indebtedness to the Columbia network and the Hollywood Hotel sponsor for permitting them to hear it again.
>
> In considering Dickens an author who is ageless, I feel it a great honor to have been selected to play the role of Scrooge at Christmastime, and if there is any message I could add to Dickens' teachings, I would say, 'Get on speaking terms with your ghost, better known as your conscience. Make of him a friend—a friend who will be able to point out, as he did to Scrooge, the way to a happy life.'"
>
> —*The Washington Post*, December 20, 1936

(Very much an educated Twentieth Century man's Freudian/Jungian understanding of "ghosts"!)

But as these words of Lionel's were being read by the fireplace all around the country, in sunny Los Angeles the star's wife Irene Fenwick was very ill. As he tells it in his book *We Barrymores*:

> "(I was with friends) in the garden on Christmas Eve 1936, when Irene suddenly died."

Among other maladies, sources report that she suffered from what would today be diagnosed as anorexia nervosa; the Barrymores had no children, and by all accounts Lionel genuinely doted on his often-ailing wife of 12 years. *The Philadelphia Record* reported that Irene's doctor found Barrymore on his knees at her bedside, weeping, and that he remained so distraught over her death that he had to be taken to a sanatorium.

There had been some chilliness in Lionel's relationship with his brother over this marriage at first; John had dated Irene earlier, and so had disparaged the state of her chastity to Lionel. But after a few years, that breach had been repaired. And so:

> "I was supposed to go on the radio in 'A Christmas Carol' the next day. With hardly a moment to read through the lines in advance, Jack took my place and gave that memorable performance which perhaps you recall."

The day after, *The Washington Post* reported that:

> "Lionel Collapses, But a Barrymore Acts as 'Scrooge'....And so it was the voice of John that recited the memorable lines of Dicken's [*sic*] 'Christmas Carol' over a nation-wide broadcast...."

Speaking of voices, it is a pity that this program does not appear to exist in recorded form, because there is probably more than one reason why some might have recalled it as "memorable." John idolized his older brother, and as Sir Toby Belch in the transcription of his 1937 *Streamlined Shakespeare* broadcast of "Twelfth Night," he can be heard to mimic Lionel lovingly and well. The present author has always surmised that he did that in this role, too, and was gratified to find that author Margot Peters in her book *The House of Barrymore* maintains that that was indeed the case. As she told me recently:

> "Where I got the info that John imitated Lionel, I can't tell you at this date—I was

John Barrymore at the mike a few months after going on as understudy for his brother in 1936's *A Christmas Carol*, here seen appearing in his own *Streamlined Shakespeare* series.

researching the book in the 1980s. But the story goes that no listener knew that Lionel did not read *Christmas Carol* that day, because John did a dead-on imitation of his brother's Scrooge. I'd say that John did it to show that he could—'I can do what Lionel does any day!' That sort of attitude, as a kind of stunt."

And Lionel would be called on in a similar capacity just a few years later. Though unwell from decades of severe alcoholism, John was a comic regular on a popular variety show in 1942, and at a rehearsal on May 19, he collapsed. Again, from Lionel's book:

> "'The show must go on' is a hackneyed phrase, but it means something to old actors. I took Jack's place on the Rudy Vallee show on the evening of Thursday, May 21st, and though my voice and heart were heavy, I did the best I could, as Jack had done for me that Christmas after my wife died."

The younger Barrymore died just days after the Vallee broadcast.

When Christmas rolled around again in 1937, *Hollywood Hotel* featured the *Carol* again, but added to their previous year's gift to their listeners. MGM offered a sixty-minute preview version of their upcoming *Adventures of Tom Sawyer* film with Tommy Kelly and Jackie Moran, followed by forty-five minutes of Lionel Barrymore Scrooging about.

(Collector's Corner, 1937 edition: There is in circulation a recording of a twenty-nine minute *Carol* that is sometimes identified as being produced for RCA/NBC Thesaurus Syndication, and aired on December 25, 1937. To this listener's ears, its features a Los Angeles cast, and the production does sound as if it dates from that era. But some sources maintain that what is claimed to be the 1931 recording discussed in the earlier Collector's Corner may in fact be the 1937 Thesaurus production. Adding to the complication, this same twenty-nine minute recording was re-edited and syndicated by C.P. MacGregor in 1950. So we will leave all these recordings in a "semi-orphan" status until better confirmation of details.)

Campbell's Soup's sponsorship of the Yuletide special event on CBS continued. And after the publicity bonanza created on Halloween of 1938 when Orson Welles and his Mercury Theatre "dress(ed) up in a sheet and jump(ed) out of a bush and (said) Boo" to America with their "War Of The Worlds," the company had picked up that series as well. So come Christmas, Campbell's planned to offer their old gifts in a new package: *The Campbell Playhouse* (Orson Welles, producer) would present Lionel Barrymore in "A Christmas Carol."

But, like one of the sponsor's soups, the off-stage plot thickened over time...

Impressed no doubt by the radio success one of the biggest members of their stable of "more stars than there are in heaven," MGM studios had planned a film version of Dickens' classic for him—but the star's recurring hip ailment flared up again. Not wanting to let the project die (some say, because of the story's uplifting nature as war clouds gathered in Europe), Barrymore is said to have recommended British character actor Reginald Owen for the role.

The film was shot, and MGM hoped to promote it and its star on their in-house radio program, NBC's *Maxwell House presents Good News of 1939* (though it was 1938; the title of this Depression-Era program was regularly updated to look hopefully ahead to each coming year.) So Barrymore was paid *not* to play the part he was known for. But he did narrate, as he had for the film's trailer.

Host Robert Young introduces Dickens' tale enthusiastically; and from the cast of the film, Gene Lockhart and Kathleen Lockhart (real-life spouses) are warm as the Cratchits, and Ann Rutherford (who passed away as this book was being written) is a uniquely sweet Christmas Past. But beyond that this *Carol* is not all "good news" as promised.

As he had in the movie, Owen presents on mike a strangely lackluster Scrooge. And the overall production is very weak: the poor *Carol* is crammed into a twenty minute segment of the one-hour variety show; and at that, shoehorned into an ill-fitting setting of broad comedy sketches. The script is very much an adaptation of the film, rather than of Dickens' text, and carries over the flaws of its model. Among them, it has Scrooge proclaim that "I *love* Christmas!" before he even meets the last Ghost; and yet after that premature softening, we do not even get to see the poor man's full redemption—the story *ends* with Ebenezer's pleas to Christmas Future at his gravesite!

Over at CBS, since Barrymore had agreed not to compete with MGM's Scrooge by playing the role for Campbell's, their boy genius Orson Welles took on the role, apologizing during his curtain call for Barrymore's absence. (This may be where the legend began in Old Time Radio fandom that Barrymore had been too ill to perform the role.)

As per the Mercury's usual standards, the 1938 production is good overall. The script differs interestingly from the norm: it opens with the Nativity story from Luke's Gospel, and contains some portions of Dickens' text that are rarely employed in dramatizations; the merry flights with Christmas Present are fuller than usual. Alas, in an attempt to "radio-ize" the piece, the Ghost of Christmas Yet to Come is given spoken dialogue! To this listener, that weakens the character—I believe Dickens meant the Future to be as generally silent towards Scrooge as it is to all of us. And Orson Welles' Scrooge was not only likely disappointing to listeners used to Lionel Barrymore's wonderful characterization, it is far from the young actor's own shining hour. The twenty-three-year-old sounds like he's doing a stock college play or comic opera "Old Man."

To be fair, the present author's dear friend, ex-"Lucky Charms Leprechaun" Arthur Anderson, feels a bit differently:

> "I thought Orson doubled well as Scrooge and as Narrator. His Bible reading at the top, I think sets the mood; it's not particularly relevant, but yet it is. And it's a beautiful performance, beautifully low key. (Now, not all of Orson's radio performances were sterling.... He was self-indulgent from time to time—as when I heard him in Booth Tarkington's "Clarence," playing a 17-year-old boy. It was embarrassing!)"

Arthur knows whereof he speaks—he was present at the creation of the 1938 Campbell's *Carol*. He recalls:

> "I had been in radio since age eleven—in fact, one early memory I have is from station WHN in New York when I played Scrooge in a modernized version of *A Christmas Carol*! And a part of my adventure in radio of which I take great pride was being with Orson Welles.

> I first acted with Orson in 1936, when I played the lead in a program called *Peter Absolute*, about the adventures of a little boy on the Erie Canal. And less than a year and a half later I was working *for* him, as the boy Lucius in his stage *Julius Caesar*. Well, this opened to raves in November 1937, and so CBS gave Orson a radio contract. "Treasure Island" was the second one done that August of 1938, in which I played Jim Hawkins. I also played the boy Clarence in an excerpt from "Life With Father," and when they did "Sherlock Holmes" I was Billy the post boy. And then on December 23rd, '38, I was cast as the Ghost of Christmas Past.
>
> Now I was surprised at this because I was 16 years old then, still a little bit young to play a ghost—but Dickens describes the Ghost of Christmas Past as a young ghost, and gives his appearance. I was delighted to play the part."

(Dickens wrote, "…like a child: yet not so like a child as like an old man, viewed through some supernatural medium." As to the Mercury's writing in 1938:)

> "They would get together in Reuben's Restaurant which was a twenty-four hour Deli, and they would argue over the script and the food and put together the next week's radio show right there. It was a God-awful way to do it, but the results were in general, I think, brilliant. (I wasn't smart enough to keep my radio scripts; I wish now that I had.)
>
> These shows were done in Studio 1, which was CBS's largest studio. It was on the twenty-second

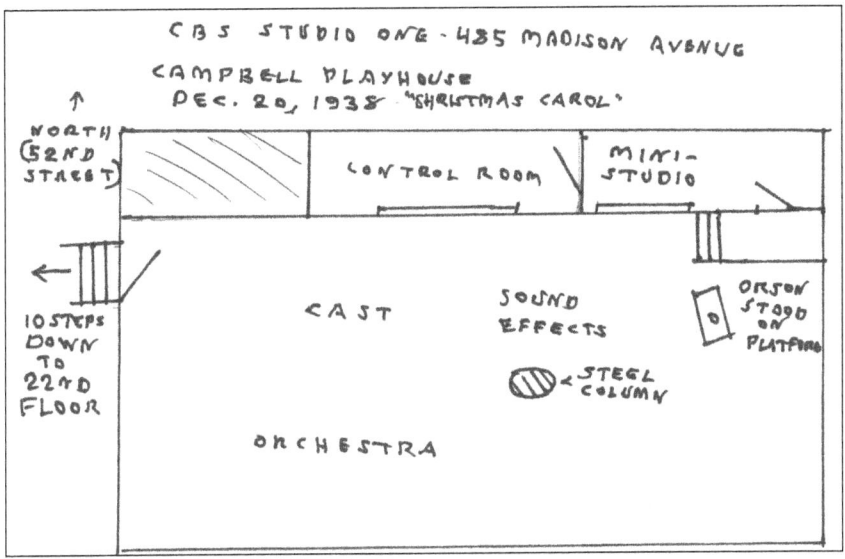

Diagram of CBS's Studio 1 by Arthur Anderson, 2012.
(Courtesy of Arthur Anderson.)

floor of 485 Madison Avenue and, on the twenty-first floor were Studios 3 and 5. But in order to have high enough ceilings so they would get the proper sound balance, Studio 1 had to be not on the twenty-second floor, but on the twenty-second-and-a-half floor—you had to climb up ten steps from the twenty-second floor. (I can only imagine the hell it was when they had to cart up or down a grand piano or a sound console!) And there was just one door at the top of those steps—then at the far east end of the studio was another door, where you went up two steps into sub-control room, which could be used as a miniature studio for echo effects."

(There does appear to be some filtering of the Ghosts in the production; and Alfred Shirley likely spent some time in that small room, because his Marley is noticeably echoed.)

"And through that room, was the control

room. But Orson didn't direct from there—he directed standing on a podium in the studio."

(About rehearsals: many accounts say that Welles did not actually run the radio ones himself?)

"This one he did. He was Scrooge, after all—he wasn't going to have Dick Wilson play Scrooge. No, he was very heavily involved with this. He was never not there.

Rehearsal was all day. After the cold read they would start working on integrating the sound effects with the script, and only after hours of that did we get to a dress rehearsal."

(About the company:)

"Hiram Sherman (Bob Cratchit): Chubby was well liked by all the actors he worked with. He had two personalities: an innocent, and a clever wit. And he was a damn good actor—he did so many Broadway musicals, and was very versatile. He and I later became great friends. I have nothing but good memories of him.

Joseph Cotten, (Nephew Fred): He and Orson liked each other and I'm sure that's why they worked together so well. Joe was one of the busiest radio actors around, and Orson was lucky to get him because Joe had so many conflicts. In Orson's early days when he was doing Works Progress Administration Theater, he wanted Joe for some of his shows, but he was not eligible because people who worked for the WPA had to be unemployed—and

Joe Cotten was very much employed. So when he did *Dr. Faustus*, Orson couldn't give him billing—so the program reads 'First Scholar played by Joseph WOOLL'!

Ray Collins (Charity Gentleman): Among his many other shows, Ray Collins had been in my *Peter Absolute*. An actor who was very versatile, very talented, and a pleasure to work with.

Alfred Shirley (Marley's Ghost): He was one of the best actors around and very, very seldom did he have anything in radio that was equal to his talents.

Kingsley Colton (Tiny Tim): Kingsley and I worked on *Let's Pretend* for years; He was even younger than I.

Alice Frost (Charwoman): All I'd heard her do was leading ladies in daytime serials, where I'd worked with her. Her Washer Woman here was so different, it impressed me."

(It's show business legend that some players—Lionel Barrymore supposedly among them—aren't the biggest fans of child actors. Were these veterans all welcoming of young Arthur Anderson?)

"The ones that I've spoken of here, yes. And we were paid the same as the adults when it came to the Mercury…probably $75?"

(These were live broadcasts—while you were waiting to go on, what was going through your mind, what were you doing?)

"Waiting for my cue. Looking forward to my appearance. But also following the story (I

The Mercury Theater in Studio 1. From right: front, Dan Seymour, Richard Wilson, Arthur Anderson (seated), William Alland; back, Orson Welles, Bernard Herrmann. Here they are rehearsing "Treasure Island," six months before "A Christmas Carol." (Courtesy of Arthur Anderson.)

> don't believe I had read it before?) at the same time, because it was such wonderful make believe. I learned more from radio, than from almost from anything else—and that included 'A Christmas Carol.'"

(Anna Stafford, who plays Young Belle, makes one little line fluff during the broadcast. If actors did that, were you chastised about it afterwards?)

> "Usually not chastised, no—but if there were too many of them, the director just didn't call you again."

(What of the "George Spelvin" that Welles lists in the cast at the end?)

> "When one actor played more than one part,

the other part was always listed as having been played by George Spelvin."

(It sounds to this author like Eustace Wyatt [Christmas Present] is doubling as Joe, the Pawnbroker; and though he's not credited in other sources, it appears to be Edgar Barrier playing Belle's Husband. And one more cast note: William Nadel reports that he was told by Welles' personal assistant at this time, Bill Herz, that he had a line or two in this production. Orson evidently made sure that was the case in many of the 1938 Mercury broadcasts, in order that Herz's salary would be paid by Campbell's/CBS, rather than by Welles himself!
And what about Arthur Anderson's performance?)

> "Looking back, I think I did a good job. But I never thought about that, then. All I thought about was the enjoyment, the pleasure and the satisfaction I got out of being in this wonderful storybook production. I think it was good casting. They had confidence in what I could do. I did very unusual things on *Let's Pretend*—from that very same studio, as a matter of fact. But I never expected to do anything like this. I was just incredibly lucky."

(And Bernard Herrmann's contribution?)

> "Wonderful music. I recognized a transition piece that's called 'The Shepherd's Hey'—'Hey' means dance, a shepherd's dance. And the juxtaposition of the voices was marvelous—the singers with the actors, and their use as part of the 'curtain' between the scenes. Bernard Herrmann had a full orchestra with us in the studio, you know—it must have been at least twelve to fifteen pieces. And there was always some timpani hanging

> around, some kettle drums or something. But over in one corner of the studio was a drum that consisted of a frame about six feet square. All one skin—God knows what kind of animal it was! A wooden frame, and the thing would just lean against the wall. I can imagine you could get some wonderful effects banging on that. It was always in the studio and I loved it. I guess I played with it a couple of times—one of the things that I loved most about Studio 1!"

(How about family or friends? Did people say "Oh, I listened to you the other night, Arthur"?)

> "I don't recall that happening. The satisfaction of doing it—that was the greatest thing. That was greater than any compliments would have been. You know, this whole adventure of 'A Christmas Carol' was such a kaleidoscope of so many wonderful sensations that it's hard to separate one from another, my mind was in a whirl! And I'm just so lucky that today, I have a recording of it. And, of course, I have to mention that in Christmas of 2010, Western Carolina University decided to do a revival of this very show...."

More on that one in future pages, Mr. Ghost of Christmas Past.

A few words about the interconnectedness in the world of the *Carols*: not only did Arthur Anderson perhaps narrowly miss working with Barrymore on this broadcast in 1938; by a strange coincidence, he had nearly been part of the famous Scrooge's 1937 edition as well. Arthur had originally been cast as the lead in the film *The Adventures of Tom Sawyer* which was previewed on that edition, but lost the part by outgrowing it during production delays. For the further adventures of Arthur Anderson, who as of this writing continues to act in his ninetieth year, see his autobiography, *An*

Actor's Odyssey. There you'll hear of a reunion with Orson Welles in Shakespeare, TV work with Joan Crawford, touring the Broadway musical *1776*, and much more.

One more point about this 1938 *Carol*, related to St. Loekle's sermon in 1933 about righteous script adaptation:

In December of 1938, the Mercury Theatre on the Air had only been under Campbell's aegis for a short time. As the sponsor had a longstanding *Carol* tradition, is it possible that Campbell's requested that Orson's group use "their" text, or that Welles & Co. welcomed it as a pre-existing work saver? That might explain the added gospel introduction that Arthur spoke of, because the 1937 *Carol* had only been a forty-five minute script. Then perhaps by the next year the Mercury had the pull, or simply chose, to do their own fresh adaptation. In fact, the 1939 edition does flow better as an audio play.

And it does much more that just that—among radio *Carol*s, it is The Big One!

The Christmas Eve 1939 *Campbell Playhouse* presentation of Charles Dickens' "A Christmas Carol," narrated by Orson Welles and featuring his Mercury Theatre company, starring Lionel Barrymore as Ebenezer Scrooge, was the performance mentioned in the Introduction that made the present author's teenage Christmases brighter, and helped to introduce him to the wonders of the medium called the Theater of the Imagination. It probably did that for many others as well, because it is one of the best-known broadcasts from the Golden Age of American Radio Drama, having been circulated by repeated broadcasting, as well as by way of reel-to-reel tape, vinyl record, audiocassette, CD, and web-stored mp3 file.

And it is one of the most *beloved* vintage *Carol*s, too, because it is quite wonderful. In a run that would eventually span twenty years, it is the most famous of all of Lionel Barrymore's performances as the "squeezing, wrenching, grasping, scraping, clutching, covetous, old sinner."

The broadcast was welcomed with much fanfare. *The Charleston Daily Mail* proclaimed on Christmas Eve that it would "…bring one of the drama's noblest names to Columbia's Christmas caravan in one of the greatest stories by one of the world's greatest writers…."

When Barrymore's Scrooge returned to CBS in 1939, the network shot a new set of publicity photos; like the first from 1935, they would be much used in the future. Note that the man holds two canes in his hands—Ebenezer would brook no such extravagance, but at this point Lionel needed them due to the hip ailment that would eventually leave him wheelchair bound. (CBS photo.)

And this *Carol* does justice to the richness of the story, with its one-hour length making it one of the two or three longest of all of Barrymore's performances of the tale. The script, likely by the Mercury's chief radio scribe Howard Koch, gracefully adapts Dickens' text, as well as artfully inventing some dialogue and business that opens up the first scene a bit from the prose story's largely descriptive beginning.

To this listener, Orson Welles was equaled as a Storyteller in the network radio era only by Jackson Beck. And his narration here is spellbinding—much more so than the year before, perhaps because his focus was split then by his doubling in the lead. Dickens' "...and I am standing in the spirit at your elbow..." line that I took for the title of this book is grippingly delivered by him, and stands as a descriptive statement of the power of audio drama itself.

Our old friend Ernest Chappell from the 1926 *Carol* mentioned earlier does his usual highly personable job as announcer, and the Mercury actors are all in fine form. Everett Sloane is pained and paining as Marley's Ghost (and doubles well as Young Scrooge, I believe); Frank Readick is meek and mild as Bob Cratchit, with Bea Benederet the backbone of the family as his wife; Ray Collins is an avuncular Charity Gentleman; and Georgia Backus, Erskine Sanford, George Coulouris, and all hands simply play the Dickens out of the story.

Bernard Herrmann's score is cheering, rousing, and frightening by turn, and is well played by his "band of merry melodians;" and the effects by sound artist Harry Essman and crew are as good as they get, in this era when Welles and his cast and company were in the very forefront of those bringing the art of radio drama to its peak.

Above all, the "Classic '39" production has that wonderful, ineffable quality described by veteran actor William Gillette (the stage's first Sherlock Holmes) in 1913 as "the illusion of the first time." By dint of excellent acting, direction, and production, the story truly unfolds for its audience as if just now happening as they listen, rather than being reenacted in arid tones from unapproachable holy writ.

Welles' introduction to this show stated that "'A Christmas Carol'... has long been a classic...and Mr. Lionel Barrymore's appearance in it is rapidly becoming one...." And as for the appellation "the best loved actor of our time" here bestowed by Orson upon Lionel, the actor demonstrates why that was so. His Scrooge is wonderfully formed, from the first rant in his office Christmas Eve to the last playful tweak of Bob's nose there the next morning, building from genuine emotion to heartbreaking terror in the gripping climax in that "church yard overrun by grass and weeds, and choked with too much burying."

The 1939 Mercury Theatre production of "A Christmas Carol" is quite simply one of the finest adaptations of the story ever, in any medium. If you haven't heard it, give yourself a wonderful Christmas gift next Yuletide!

The 1939 production was apparently not broadcast from the same New York studio that Arthur Anderson described for the 1938 show, but rather from Welles' new base of operations as he began his film career, Los Angeles. All of Barrymore's previous *Carol*s had originated there, and Orson and several of the Mercury players had moved to California earlier in 1939. Sources state that Welles had stopped commuting back to New York for the Campbell's show by October of that year; and *Variety*, which regularly posted NY-LA-NY transits by then, lists none for either Welles or Barrymore at this time.

But the newspaper does note that Campbell's executive Diana Bourbon came west for their *Carol* in 1940, when Dickens' ghost story of Christmas would become the only story ever presented twice on the Playhouse. Again, the broadcast was highly anticipated; the writer in the *Wisconsin State Journal* saying that it was, "...the real 'must' in drama...a radio tradition," just as Welles has described it the Yule before. And the newspaperman cited another reason to tune in:

> "There is a possibility that Lionel will not be physically fit, but even if he should broadcast from a wheelchair, you'll hear an incomparable Scrooge. He may not try to do it again."

After only a few short years, Barrymore's *Carol*s already had the chief hallmarks of a deeply held tradition: the expectation of the repeating of it, and the fear that it might be lost.

And indeed, the 1940 broadcast fulfilled the five-year contract for the role that the star had signed with the Columbia Broadcasting System in 1935. But other Networks would be only too happy to pick up a property that by this time had become as hot as a Christmas bowl of smoking bishop.

So in 1941 and 1942 it was the National Broadcasting Company's turn. On popular singer-bandleader-actor Rudy Vallee's *Sealtest Show*, they presented what had become by then a certified Christmas favorite. In its radio listing, the Wisconsin State Journal ranked Barrymore's performance with "King George VI's Christmas message…(as) among radio's gifts to its listeners Thursday."

(Even so, Lionel had some worthy competition for the Scroogestakes during Yuletide 1941. More on that in the next chapter.)

In the 1941 *Carol* Lionel is joined by his castmate from the film *Test Pilot*, Dix Davis; he would be a Cratchit Boy again in the second Vallee broadcast of the story the following year. Fellow child actor Tommy Cook worked with Davis in a different 1942 *Carol* that we will cover in the next chapter, and recalls him as, "the best all-around child actor from the West Coast—brilliant." Other members of a sort of informal "Radio *Carol* Stock Company" that formed over the years who are present in this show include Lou Merrill (who Cook also describes as brilliant, adding "great memories of working with him!"), Barbara Jean Wong, Eric Snowden, and Alec Harford. Reprising her role of Mrs. Cratchit from the 1938 broadcast and movie, Kathleen Lockhart is joined here as there by daughter June.

And in the lead, Barrymore turns in a vigorous performance, his voice having much of the same dark heaviness as found in his 1939 performance for Campbell's.

The half-hour Campbell's script from 1940 is not available for comparison, but this one of the same length from the next year is a distinct drop in quality from the Classic '39 one-hour. Already short, it is hurt additionally by time lost to the show's introduction, commercials, and closing; there is almost no segue in or out of the Ghosts' scenes; and the latter portion cuts directly from Tim's death to Scrooge's grave. As often seems to be the case, the Cratchit Dinner scene is left the fullest, and played the best—likely those involved sensed its centrality to the story.

Barrymore speaks elsewhere of an evolution of his *Carol* scripts down through the years, and there are some continuities to be found. Here, something from the 1939 Welles production is carried over: as the opening Office Scene ends, the narrator happily tells us that, "Cratchit ran home, to play Christmas games with his loving family…"—and then there is an ominous musical sting telegraphing

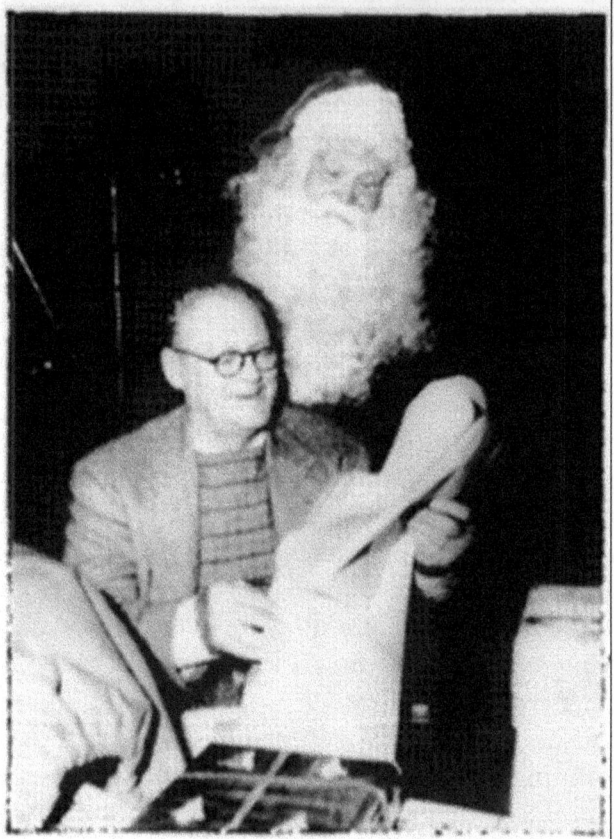

Newspaper radio page note for Rudy Vallee's 1942 *Carol*, which also mentions Barrymore's previous Christmas offering on his own series that week.

the shift in tone to—"...Scrooge, on the other hand...went home to...his banker's book." Did this effective moment originate with the Mercury's musical whiz, Bernard Herrmann, and was it carried over by Lionel, who appreciated it as a composer himself?

As for our 1941 host, though some sources claim that Vallee plays Bob in the show, he in fact narrates the piece. And although he does not attempt a British accent (many actors don't in these vintage American productions; in fact Barrymore himself generally goes only so far as Mid-Atlantic), he does a competent job. But interestingly, though Vallee was said by some employees to be a bit of a Scrooge himself as he was a hard-driving perfectionist unforgiving of error, the singer can be heard to make several very noticeable mistakes in the lyrics of the carols sung during the broadcast!

In 1942, in addition to doing his second NBC *Carol*, Barrymore moonlighted in a modern Wartime variation on the theme. The syndicated *Treasury Star Parade* program "A Modern Scrooge," was hosted by Fredric March, later to be an early TV Scrooge himself. And in this one, a town crank refuses to buy Bonds—until a Ghost shows him his nephew's peril on the battlefield, for want of the bullets that his money would have bought. Lionel here creates a character different from his Ebenezer Scrooge, and as "Jeb Kreaker," proves again that of himself, his brother, and his sister, he was the only one of the famous Philadelphian theatrical threesome who could convincingly portray a rural American Midwesterner.

Following its two years in the Vallee, 1943 saw the *Carol* presented within the framework of Barrymore's own weekly half-hour series, *The Mayor of the Town*. Then in its second season, this "situation dramedy" would remain the story's home through 1947. First carried over CBS, the show later moved to the fledgling American Broadcasting Company (which itself had spun off from NBC in 1943), granting Barrymore's Scrooge a debut on that network. Two *Mayor* Carols are in circulation, and their scripts differ in tone from Barrymore's earlier broadcasts; perhaps written by that program's seasoned radio scribe Jean Holloway, their phrasing and rhythm seem a bit more homogenized into the contemporary series episode form.

And how was the quality of work of the star himself? Lionel Barrymore was named "Best Actor of 1942–1943" in a poll of

Most famed Barrymore radio roles in twenty years on air have been as "Mayor of the Town" (above with Agnes Moorehead as Marilly), Scrooge in "A Christmas Carol"

Two of radio's best actors, Lionel Barrymore and Agnes Moorehead—for eight years on *Mayor of the Town* both Mayor and Housekeeper, and Miser and Mrs. Cratchit.

national radio listeners, based largely on his annual *Carol*s and the *Mayor* series.

Let's consider the next several paragraphs as a "Collector's Corner, 1942-3 edition—*plus*...."

There is an Armed Forces Radio Service edited *Mayor* Carol in circulation dated 1942. The present author believes that is likely a mistake, as newspapers for Christmas of 1942 confirm Lionel's *Carol* on Vallee's show again that year, with "a Christmas Party" on his own *Mayor* series. (See caption to the previous photo.) It may be the one from 1943, as the announcer in the transcription says that we are returning to "...a Christmas Eve *one hundred* years ago...," which takes us to the year when Dickens' book was published. And just for the record, that announcer is Frank Martin, though the series' regular was Harlow Wilcox.

The other *Mayor* Carol in circulation is from AFRS as well: a *Globe Theater* hosted by Herbert Marshall that is variously dated as either from 1944 or 1947. As with the 1942 *Mayor* Carol listed above, the narrator is Frank Martin; and to this listener's ears, the show also features Agnes Moorehead as Mrs. Cratchit and Joe Kearns (of TV's *Dennis the Menace*) as Christmas Past.

Whichever year it dates from, this production is graced with very nice musical underscoring and transitions, but sadly the script is not one of the better of Lionel's many half-hour productions. The necessary cuts are not well-chosen: there is no confrontation with Cratchit leaving the office, and when (again, a *speaking*!) Future appears, he takes Scrooge directly to his gravesite, granting no buildup to the climax. And other changes do not help either: Present wakes Scrooge with a whisper at his bedside, instead of the much stronger moment of bidding him into his greens-bedecked sitting room with boisterous call; and early on, Scrooge in his childhood flashback scene uncharacteristically tells his harsh schoolmaster that, "Christmas is very important…to a child…."

But the acting is very good. Barrymore brings more dark humor to his Scrooge than before—he shows as much cynical superiority to others, as anger. It's a valid choice for the character, in some ways stronger than simple ranting; George C. Scott would take a similar tack in his TV Movie version forty years later. And Agnes Moorehead brings a real sharpness to her Mrs. Cratchit this year, at times reminiscent of her spinster aunt in the 1942 film *The Magnificent Ambersons*.

The December 25, 1944, issue of *Life* magazine features a wonderful seven-page spread promoting Barrymore accompanied by a text proclaiming that:

> "…millions of Americans who have forsaken the old custom of reading the Carol aloud to the children on Christmas Eve, would hardly consider Christmas to be Christmas without hearing Barrymore harrumph and growl his way through the role of old Scrooge…."

The Ghost of Christmas Future (Francis Stevens) confronts Ebenezer Scrooge (Lionel Barrymore.) (*Life* magazine, 1944.)

The portfolio of fully-cast, fully-staged pictures shot on the MGM lot is a tantalizing "what if?" look at what a Barrymore Scrooge film would have been like.

In another example of the synergy among *Carol*s down through the years, the last picture in the series, showing the reformed Scrooge reading to a Tiny Tim seated on his lap, was later the basis for the beautiful painted cover on the 1947 set of 78 rpm records which preserved Barrymore's *Carol* for home listening.

Just for the record, sources show that starting during this period there was sometimes more than one Barrymore miser per Yule haunting the airwaves, with both live and ghostly rebroadcast shows.

And so "Lionel Scrooge" marched on.

The publishers of a contemporary Garden City reprint of Dickens' novel presented this paean to the star as Foreword:

> "Four years ago A Christmas Carol appeared on a radio program...critical to begin with, (those who tuned in) were prepared to be resentful of any liberties taken with their beloved story.... That the radio presentation at Christmas has become one of the most popular fixtures of the air, is due almost entirely to the sympathetic genius of Lionel Barrymore whose 'Scrooge' is so incomparably right that the tale takes on new luster in his telling of it."

The wonderful full-color illustrations of Scrooge by Everett Shinn that grace the book are clearly meant to suggest a slightly gaunter version of the actor. And in the Introduction, Barrymore again shared some of his own feelings about the character and the story:

> "To contemplate Charles Dickens' *A Christmas Carol* is to stand in awe before a mighty edifice of heroism and cowardice, anchored deep in the soil of all humanity. Its pinnacle is the homemade crutch of Tiny Tim, bright in a fluorescent beam of tenderness which touches heaven; while far below, in subterranean darkness, at the foundation a human termite bores at the shoring timbers of charity....
>
> There is something I feel of Scrooge at the moment I assume his character. I seem to shrink, and an unnatural meanness of disposition comes upon me. The transition is rapid, and I go out into the city Scrooge in body and mind, an actor's privileged metamorphosis. That remaining remnant that is still myself (at least enough of it remaining to direct me to the radio [*sic*] or the theater in which I have contracted to appear) grows increasingly wary and uncomfortable....

I open the stage door in the face of a beaming and solicitous,

'Good evening, Mr. Barrymore.'

'Barrymore? Who is Barrymore? Scoundrel!' I snarl. The ragged children at the stage door call after me, 'Merry Christmas, Mister Scrooge!'....

'Bah, ye leeches, ye wasters, spenders! Yer plight's of yer own makin'. Away with ye, let me pass! Ye'll get nothin' out of me!'

'We'll wait,' is chorused after me as I slam the door....

(Then) Scrooge is at the microphone, and there, Marley's phantom-messenger points his bony finger while, like a gust of wind along a gutter's edge, comes his voice. 'Christmas past, Christmas present, Christmas yet to come.'

****

"(At the end of it), as I back away from the microphone in the thunderous peal of the rollicking bells, my spirit lifts up out of the weight of pounds, shillings, and pence, flees the cramped, thin body of Scrooge, and leaps to catch up with the joyous spirit of the day. What little of the miserly Scrooge remains is wrung out of me by the handshakes of those about me on the stage.

It's Christmas and Scrooge is no more, his pinched-thin, miserly stoop has left my body; I breathe more easily, less stingily; my step is lighter and my heart is lifted.

I wish to shower coins on the children in the theater alleyway, but as I go to the radio station as the miser Scrooge, I play that part and carry not a penny. Now I am confronted with the embarrassing expedient of borrowing from my friends; even the stage doorman unloads his purse for me to scatter among the children who had wished—even Scrooge—a Merry Christmas."

With that, a few words here about Lionel Barrymore the man, both the external and the internal, seem fitting. First, what did he look like on the *outside*, when playing the scenes he just described?

Several sources, including Hollis Alpert in his book *The Barrymores*, claim that the actor did his radio performances as Scrooge in costume. The present author can hear many Old Time Radio fans howling at that idea, and finds it a little hard to credit himself; such dressing for the mike was almost unheard of in those days. But the operative word there is, "almost."

There were exceptions. Ed Wynn's "Fire Chief," for one, and Fanny Brice's "Baby Snooks," for another. So with a legendary actor in an iconic role, in productions often done before a live audience, *maybe* there were occasions when Barrymore's Scrooge faced the audience in the Victorian garb seen in his *Carol* publicity photos. But for the record, one of his Tiny Tims, Stuffy Singer (who we'll hear more from later) says "no," at least in the case of his show.

And what was Lionel Barrymore like on the *inside*, in the years that he played this role?

In his book introduction quoted just above, his newspaper essay we looked at earlier, and another piece that we'll come to in a while, the actor speaks of how he felt about Scrooge—especially the sunny, redeemed Scrooge of that glorious Christmas morning. Did he understand, too, the darker miser that we first meet one frightening Christmas Eve?

Following are some more words from the man's autobiography. First, concerning the time of his first marriage, which failed:

> "If (the reader has) hung on this far, he has tried to stick confused clues together and determine what manner of person this Barrymore really is. I am trying to indicate throughout that I am an unusually nice fellow, but I perceive that some of the evidence is against me.
>
> Not to excuse myself for anything but simply to set down what seems to me to be true, I suppose that my frustrations as a painter, my preoccupation with music, and my obsession with the idea that I wanted to escape from the theater contributed toward making me a difficult person to live with. These and all the other weaknesses and instabilities which may mark even persons of the highest good will—and none of us in our hearts ever doubts his own essential good will—made me abrupt, made me thankless, made me thoughtless, made me sour."

And then, about his physical ills:

> "I admire men who can meet misfortune with a stiff British lip or a 'Heigh Ho!' but I am not one of this breed. In adversity I dree my weird with full diapason, keen like a crone at a hanging, and call pitifully upon the gods to drop all nonessential affairs and give me their full attention."

Adversity: for years, the broken hip that never properly healed caused Lionel great pain. It also led to a serious drug dependency and the inability to move about freely. Arthur Anderson tells this story:

"In 1945, I was traveling from service duty in Idaho and Texas to Hawaii on my way overseas. I had a break while passing through Los Angeles, and met up there with one of the first radio producers who had used me back in New York, Knowles Entriken. He was then doing *Mayor of the Town*, and told me of one occasion when the cast all left for supper break before the show, and Mr. Barrymore was left all alone in the studio in his wheelchair... The microphone had been left on, and in the control room they could hear him express his frustration by mumbling

'...F@*&K everybody...!'"

The Bard might have said that Lionel suffered "the heart-ache and the thousand natural shocks that flesh is heir to" but that "he was a man, take him for all in all." Every really good actor uses their Self as the clay from which to sculpt the characters they create, and out of this man Lionel Barrymore came a living, breathing Ebenezer Scrooge.

One of the very best. Ever.

And now, back to our story—with a quick sidelight by cathode ray tube:

At least as early as Dumont TV's experimental *Carol* in 1943, radio's Scrooges were beginning to have Christmas competition from the new "radio-with-pictures" variety. And for the next decade or so, the two media would vie for a slice of the Christmas (*Carol*) pie—in fact, that Dumont production had involved radio's George Lowther and Lon Clark. By Yuletide 1948, opera star Dennis King's well-received TV Scrooge for Philco would be meeting his Spirits the same weekend that Lionel Barrymore parried his as part of a special radio extravaganza. And speak of going into the belly of the beast—his 1949 radio Carol was sponsored by TV manufacturer Capehart!

In fact, we may have only barely missed a video Scrooge from Lionel: it is said the actor wanted to work in the new medium, but

Strange days indeed in 1949: a television manufacturer sponsors a radio *Carol*!

was discouraged by his long-standing film contract with MGM's Louis B. Mayer.

But on the radio, still a fixture in many more homes than that newfangled box, his role as an essential part of the nation's Christmas continued by way of radio through the Forties.

In 1946, The Associated Press announced that "(for the) Christmas season...two features...have become fixtures, Lionel Barrymore as Scrooge in Dickens' 'A Christmas Carol,' and Kate Smith's 'The Small One'...." And in 1947, The Racine *Journal-Times* expressed even more strongly the sentiment that was shared by many Americans:

> "Christmas without Santa Claus, holly wreaths, and beloved Lionel Barrymore taking the part of Scrooge in Dickens' Christmas Carol would be a sorry Yuletide indeed."

The bond between Barrymore and his listeners had been forged in the Yuletide fire during a decade where they had shared a Great Depression and a World War. Perhaps the story is true that he'd encouraged MGM to go forward without him on their filmed *Carol* precisely because of what Dickens' story meant during such hard times.

In fact in 1947, Lionel was encouraged to immortalize his signature role for future generations by way of the new MGM Records company (see next chapter).

That same year, *Mayor* moved for one Fall-Spring season to ABC; it was then on hiatus over the winter, until revival by Mutual for its final Spring season in 1949. That gave CBS the chance to welcome Barrymore and his *Carol* back home in 1948 with a star-studded two-hour spectacular not unlike his debut on that net in 1934.

And in 1949, Barrymore completed his "conquest by Christmas spirit" of all the major radio networks. It was the Mutual Broadcasting System who presented *The Capehart Christmas Hour* mentioned earlier, a thirty minute *Carol* plus thirty minutes of holiday music. For the next three years, his *Carol* stayed on that network.

And it was a propitious match—to this listener's ears, the 1949 and 1950 broadcasts are excellent ones. As the actor wrote in his autobiography:

> "(Our) adaptations of Dickens' CHRISTMAS CAROL…(have) apparently become a fixture which people expect and accept because after all somebody ought to read the CAROL to children at Christmastime."

(Even President Franklin Roosevelt was known to do that for the youngsters of his family during his time in the White House in the Thirties and Forties. But he may not have been among those who gave that practice up in deference to Lionel's version—because as the actor admits in the same book, they were well known to be on opposite sides of the fence politically.)

> "An odd thing about this is that we have produced it differently from year to year, with various players and with various cuts and additions to the original, but no one has seemed to notice…."

Some of us have certainly noticed, Lionel.

As our old comrade Harold Loekle implied earlier, there is an art to compressing material without taking out its heart. And the 1949 script manages that very well indeed. True, the trimming means that the only scene with Christmas Past is the breakup with Belle, and that the story ends with a deliriously happy Scrooge telling Turkey Boy what he'll do for Bob Cratchit the next day, instead of us seeing it happen; but the words used are prime Dickens, and finishing the story on the high note of Christmas morning actually works.

And perhaps because an actor always knows and appreciates when he's working from a solid script, Lionel rises to rare form and does a fine job. And so does the rest of the cast, which includes several members of the unofficial Radio Carol Stock Company—Joseph Kearns, Eric Snowden, and Byron Kane.

And the judicious cuts leave room, in that Occupied Europe/Cold War era, for a patriotic speech by Barrymore in the coda:

> "Ya know, it's always seemed to me that the story of Ebenezer Scrooge held a moral for nations, as well as people...for if all the nations of the world will banish greed, cruelty, avarice, and selfishness, then truly it'll be a 'Happy New Year' to all the woooorld...!"

The sentiment sounds as if it comes from the heart, and knowing the actor's other comments about the piece and his feeling of responsibility towards it, it seems possible that Barrymore drafted this sign-off himself.

One that Dickens would have heartily agreed with.

The 1950 broadcast ends with a similar patriotic passage, this time, sadly, having the troops newly arrived in Korea to reference. The production uses the same script as the previous year's, and is as strong a production overall—if anything, after sixteen years Barrymore's performance in the lead is even fresher and more vigorous than the year before. And as proof of his other talents, the announcer at the end of the 1950 broadcast invites listeners to write in for a free collection of Christmas stories from *Guideposts* magazine, which contains one written by Barrymore himself.

As for the next year's broadcast, Variety's "Gros." gave it a very favorable—and very perceptive—review:

> "Mutual network launched its Yule season programming Sunday (23) in top style, choosing Charles Dickens' classic, 'A Christmas Carol,' with Lionel Barrymore in the familiar Scrooge assignment. It was Barrymore's 18th annual airing of the role."

(It was actually the sixteenth; but without exhaustive records in front of them concerning Barrymore's missed broadcast in 1936 and his narrator's role in 1938, newspaper writers of the time can be forgiven for often miscalculating his growing Scrooge tally over the rolling years.)

> "Although the tale was pared down to a half-hour's running time, its careful editing kept the stanza clear and effective. Dickens' basic message that Xmas was a time for benevolence and charity show through the script. His characters are so well drawn that they never wear out their annual visit and manage to sustain interest despite a rereading, reviewing or rehearing.
>
> Barrymore's interpretation of Scrooge has become as much a classic as the Dickens' tale. He still carries the role with sharpness and wit and is completely effective as he changes from tyrant to benefactor. Other cast members projected the story's spirit and Tiny Tim's windup 'God bless us all, everyone' was still a sock clincher."

"A sock clincher." God bless *Variety* and its clichéd showbiz lingo. But then, evidently even ST. NICK himself agreed that the Barrymore *Carol*s were boffo! (See ad on next page.)

On to 1952, where (fittingly, as it would turn out) it was back yet again to where they had started for Lionel Scrooge & Co., as CBS presented them on the *Hallmark Playhouse* that year. Not long after, the actor became the host of that series, which was soon to be rechristened the *Hallmark Hall of Fame*.

And his 1953 performance of the *Carol* there marked nineteen years since Barrymore's first essaying of the role. Simon "Stuffy" Singer, that year's Tiny Tim, speaks:

> "I remember doing three or four shows with

The Old Clauses settle down to listen to Old Scrooge. (1951)

In 1953 Lionel Barrymore returned to a regular weekly radio series, allowing him to showcase his own *Carol* as he had done during *Mayor of the Town*'s run.

Lionel Barrymore. One was the story where the little boy gets trapped up in a tree by Death, because Death is trying to take the grandfather—*On Borrowed Time.* And I think I may have actually done *A Christmas Carol* more than just this once? All probably because I remember hearing—and this was very reflected, I didn't hear it directly—that the reason that I did multiple shows with him was because he didn't generally like children, but I was okay! And that was because on basically every show that we did, my Mom and I would play catch....

Now I was born at the end of '41, so I would have been about 12 at this time. It was the downtime that was kind of dangerous for kids—hyperactive kids—and indoors she would manufacture a ball made out of paper and tape or at a movie studio she would bring gloves and a ball, and we would play catch. Athletics were a big part of my life from the time I was a little kid."

(Mr. Singer is too modest here. He has been nationally ranked in tennis, is in the handball Hall of Fame, and played football and baseball as well.)

"That was something that kept me happy, and kept me out of messing around with the instruments or the orchestra, or the—what did they call it?—the special effects guys, the sound effects folk. And I remember that when I would do a Phil Harris and Alice Faye show, which was following literally immediately after a Jack Benny show that I had done, Phil Harris would grab me by the hand and we'd run through the parking lot to go from one studio to the other!

As far as the cast of *Christmas Carol*: I knew Anne Whitfield—I'm guessing that she's a little older than I am. I worked with her a lot; I think she was in *Peter Pan*."

(Stuffy did voice work for the Disney animated feature.)

("And I think Anne was also on *Too Many Cooks*, which is one of the funnier shows you'll ever hear, if you can find it. It's Hal March, Bob Sweeney, Mary Jane Croft, Richard Crenna as the oldest child, and it goes down to me as the youngest—every kid actor you can think of was on that show, and it's hysterical!)

Herb Butterfield, wow, it seemed like he was every place. He had a little bit of a different kind of voice, if I remember correctly. And I worked with Parley Baer a lot, but I can't tell you where.

As far as Lionel Barrymore, now, remember, I was just a little kid then…I don't remember somebody rolling him around, so it could have just been a chair, but I think that he was in a wheelchair.

And as I recall, these shows were done in a big theater, I want to say on Vine Street, with an audience—and I mean a large audience."

(It was likely CBS Columbia Square on Sunset, near Vine, where NBC was.)

"And my recollection is that my Dad was

The Hollywood studios of CBS during the network radio era.

my—if you want to call it anything—my interpretation or inflection coach, and we certainly did the script many times before we went into the studio. I don't think I knew the story until such time as we started doing the script; but remember, this was something different from doing a TV show, where you could do it over and over again. With a radio show you've got to hit your mark right—now!"

And twelve-year-old Stuffy did just that. Though Tim is a very small role in this script, he is an appropriately earnest little lad.

Before we leave Mr. Singer, we should note that among his many other radio appearances is another well-remembered Christmas broadcast: the 1949 *Great Gildersleeve* episode where Hal Peary tells the story of "Why The Chimes Rang." He appeared frequently on television as well, including a stint as son Alexander in *Blondie*. And in addition to all of this performing and the athletic honors mentioned earlier, he works today in Financial Planning! Truly a "man of parts," well beyond just actors' roles.

And besides Stuffy's Tiny Tim, that other noted young *Carol* character, Turkey Boy, was played in the 1953 broadcast by twenty-six-year-old Dick Beals of *Davey and Goliath* and "Speedy Alka-Seltzer" fame. Beals had a medical condition that kept his stature small and his voice young, but he lived to the ripe old age of eighty-five, and just passed away during the writing of this book.

But alas, this *Carol* as a whole is problematic. Though 1952's is not available for comparison, the 1953 CBS script by Leonard St. Clair is a decided step down from the previous MBS ones, once again falling into the trap of exchanging weak new lines for Dickens' stronger originals—hearing Cratchit move about the office, Scrooge barks, "shall I hire you a fiddler to accompany your dancing?" Oddly, Past and Present are presented in nearly as threatening a vein as Marley; once again, mute Future speaks; and the plot is without a Fezziwig dance, a Belle, or an Old Joe! And a music score of powerful choral interludes is both interruptive of the story, and ineffective as transitions.

But good work is done by all of the seasoned radio cast including Joe Kearns as Marley, Parley Baer (later the "Keebler Elf") as Past, and John Stephenson ("Jonny Quest's" father) as narrator. And though his voice is getting a bit thick with age at seventy-five, Barrymore does yeoman like work—even after eighteen returns to the story, he does not just walk through the role. There is commitment evident, with a welcome variety from his earlier performances.

And it was to be this legendary Scrooge's final bow.

Lionel Herbert Blythe (his legal birth name) passed away at the age of seventy-six on November 16, 1954. He had been scheduled to do the *Carol* again, so Hallmark reran the transcription of the previous year's production, hosted by Edward Arnold, as a salute to the actor—and in a tribute to a truly amazing achievement in radio history. As we have seen, Barrymore had been named "Best Actor" in a 1942/43 national radio listeners' poll, based largely on his *Carol*s, and the annual visits by his Scrooge were always welcomed in the press like the return of an old friend. And he had for all intents and purposes finally presented the character on screen (without, sadly, the key redemption scene), as Old Man Potter in Frank Capra's

STAVE 3: THE SCROOGE AWAKES

THE NEW YORK TIMES

Barrymore as a Star of Stage, Screen and Radio

1918: Lionel Barrymore as he appeared in "The Copperhead" at Shubert Theatre.

1935: He had a starring role in motion picture based on book "David Copperfield."

1939: In yearly radio interpretation of Scrooge in Dickens' "A Christmas Carol."

BARRYMORE DEAD ON THE COAST AT 76

Continued From Page 1

Lionel Barrymore's obituary, noting as among the highlights of his sixty-year career the role of Ebenezer Scrooge.

holiday classic, *It's A Wonderful Life*.

It's fitting that we close the book on Lionel Barrymore's storied history with the Carol with a swansong by the man himself, from the liner notes to his 1947 record version:

> "As you know, I have played many roles during my career. But, if there is one role I really hope I'll be remembered for, it's that of Ebenezer Scrooge.
>
> Yes, Scrooge was as miserable, miserly, and

mean a character as ever lived. He was completely without faith, friends, or love, nor did he want them. And yet I have always loved the old humbug—not for what he *was*, but for what he *became*. That, to me, is not only the moral of 'A Christmas Carol,' but one of the great lessons of Christmas and life itself. It's not what a man is, but what he can become that's important. And it's never too late (or too early for that matter) to start 'becoming.'

I've played Scrooge more times than I can remember, and each time I like him—and 'A Christmas Carol'—more and more. My biggest thrill of all comes when Scrooge awakens on Christmas morning to find that he's alive... and that being alive, for the first time, is a joyous thing.

That's the Scrooge I love. The Scrooge who says, humbly, 'I will honour Christmas in my heart, and try to keep it all the year.'"

And thanks to Lionel's heartfelt work in the role over the course of many years, that was the Scrooge that AMERICA loved, too. The year after his passing, the press release for the LP reissue of his 1947 78 rpms said that, "...after Mr. Barrymore's lamented death, the recording takes on a deeper significance, preserving as it does his remarkable performance...."

Down through the years, the almost childlike giddy expectation shown in the newspapers each time a visit with Barrymore's Scrooge was approaching makes it clear that many Americans felt just as the co-author of the classic OTR tome *The Big Broadcast*, veteran announcer Bill Owen, did:

"I never missed Lionel's annual interpretation on radio—he *was* Scrooge, as surely as Basil Rathbone was Sherlock Holmes."

STAVE 4:
The Rest of the Spirits

"There was a radio show I did one Christmas morning during the war. The entire live audience in the studio was in uniform...with myself as Mr. Scrooge."

—Basil Rathbone, 1962

Of course in all those years when the Babe Ruth of radio Scrooges was hitting them out of the park every winter season, there WERE other players in the league. Many were, like Barrymore, stars in their own right. And also on the bench were many gifted radio supporting actors who were members of the Radio *Carol* Stock Company, such as Ernest Chappell, Dix Davis, Agnes Moorehead, Arthur Q. Bryan, Joe Kearns, and several others.

And some of the stars who raised up their Ebenezer in America during the reign of Lionel Barrymore actually hailed from the land of Scrooge.

One of those was Edmund Gwenn.

Born in 1877, Gwenn had an enviable theater career in England that included creating several stage roles for George Bernard Shaw, before becoming a beloved character actor during the golden age of American film. He appeared in parts ranging from a vicious assassin in Hitchcock's *Foreign Correspondent* to the archetypal 50s "Good Scientist" in *Them!*, and his versatility was well demonstrated in Yule dramas—as well as embodying Dickens' grasping old miser on the radio, he is probably best remembered today for his filmic portrayal of Santa Claus. What appears to be Gwenn's first turn as Scrooge was in a five-part *Carol* (which also seems to be the first in that serial format) over WOR/Mutual, Christmas week of 1941. Seven-year-old Ted Donaldson joined him as Tiny Tim, and by running from the 22nd to the 26th, their serial actually stole a bit of thunder from Barrymore's Vallee show turn on the 25th.

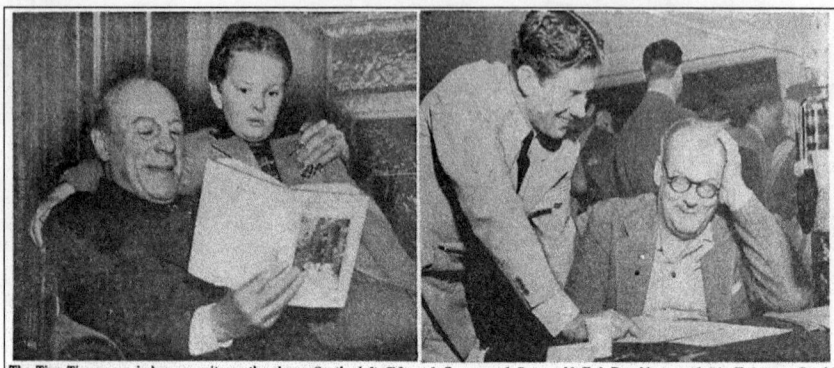

The Tiny Tim season is here, as witness the above: On the left, Edmund Gwenn and 7-year-old Ted Donaldson read "A Christmas Carol," which they will act in five episodes, Monday through Friday, 4:15 P.M. to 4:30, over WOR-Mutual. . . . At the right is Lionel Barrymore, whose reading of the Dickens classic is an annual event. He will be heard this time on the Rudy Vallee hour, on Christmas night at 10 o'clock over WEAF (NBC-Red). Here he is, talking it over with Mr. V.

Dueling Scrooges of 1941!

And Gwenn would actually *share* a venue in the role of Scrooge with a fellow member of the British Empire, South African-born Basil Rathbone.

Rathbone's career had already included Shakespeare on stage in both England and America when we began the First World War service, which resulted in being awarded the Military Cross. This was followed by more stage work, including a play with Lionel Barrymore's sister Ethel, and Silent film. His over thirty years of Sound Cinema includes such notable films as *David Copperfield, Anna Karenina, The Adventures of Robin Hood,* and *Son of Frankenstein,* but he was of course most famous in the role of Sherlock Holmes, which he would play on film, on the radio, on stage, and on television.

Rathbone first figuratively donned Scrooge's dressing gown in yet another medium, for the Columbia Records production of 1942. That season's Christmas Eve also saw a *Carol* broadcast with him on WIND Chicago, and as that city's *Daily Tribune* describes the program as being "set to music by...Leith Stevens," as well as being 25 minutes in length, two characteristics it shares with the record album, it may have been a licensed broadcast of same.

The actor followed that one with his first confirmed original-broadcast *Carol* in 1943 on CBS's *Stars Over Hollywood.* This may be the production that the actor speaks of in the quote that began this chapter, and about which he says in his autobiography, *In and Out of Character*:

> "...A Christmas Carol by Charles Dickens... was performed in the NBC Studios in Hollywood for the benefit of the men and women of the Armed Forces only. The format was charming. In a room, supposedly my home, I was sitting reading the Dickens story to my daughter Cynthia. There was a knock at the door and a friend dropped in to say 'Happy Christmas.' He apologized for interrupting, but was persuaded to stay and hear this Christmas story. I started reading again and we imperceptibly drifted into the acting version....When the play was finished I closed the book and we all wished each other and our listening audience a very happy Christmas, and my friend left. When we went off the air there was a rush for my autograph. I signed and signed and signed for quite some while, until I became conscious there was someone else's name on each piece of paper. In firm round copybook writing there it was, CYNTHIA RATHBONE! I looked up, and there *she* was in her little starched white Christmas frock signing away as if she had been my co-star, which indeed she had certainly proved to be."

Basil would not only don Scrooge's slippers again on the radio, he would also play the role very well in two television productions in the 1950s (one, a musical.) But his preference as to the two media?

> "Radio is unquestionably a superior medium to television because it makes us use our imagination."

1944 saw Rathbone Scrooging in his favored medium again, over WABC. And yet another member of "The Hollywood Raj" was also with him and Gwenn in the Christmas radio Forties fray.

"This GREATEST of Shows!"(?) Were the *Stars* folks making a dig at a certain *other* famous broadcast *Carol*? Or perhaps even hoping readers would tune in thinking that theirs actually *was* the other?

Original Christmas-red vinyl *Favorite Story* Carol transcription disc, furnished by producer/syndicator Ziv to the stations who aired the series. (Courtesy of Randy A. Riddle.)

Ronald Colman began his career on the stage and in the silent cinema in England, and soon appeared on the American stage, including Broadway. His first American film was *The White Sister* with Lillian Gish, followed by smash success in the original silent version of *Beau Geste*. He went on to even greater renown in films including *A Tale of Two Cities, Lost Horizon,* and *Random Harvest*, earning an Academy Award for his work in *A Double Life*. And in those talking films, a great asset was his justly famous smoky Anglo voice—which of course was put to good use in his many radio and audio performances.

Colman had actually beaten Basil Rathbone to the Christmas punch, first *Carol*ing the same year Edmund Gwenn did, 1941. And his warm-up was in a similar dugout to Basil's, by way of a record album production covered in the next chapter.

Favorite Story's Charity Gent, Arthur Q. Bryan, and Ebenezer Scrooge, Ronald Colman, seen here in a publicity photo for the series.

By 1946 Colman was hosting his own popular syndicated radio series, and in a special 1949 episode of *Favorite Story*, Colman ably embodied the lead in Dickens' tale.

In a rare twist, Scrooge narrates the story in the first person; but as the story is told in flashback by an already reformed miser, that and his slightly-too-mawkish closing monologue lessen the bite of the story a bit. But the actor is very ably supported by such radio veterans as Jimmy Lydon (the movies' Henry Aldrich), Joseph Kearns, Lurene Tuttle, and Arthur Q. Bryan (aka Elmer Fudd). One time "Tiny Tim" Tommy Cook, who we will hear more from soon, says about those last two fellow *Carol*ers: "Lurene Tuttle was one of the all-time radio greats; and Arthur Q. Bryan was very clever—and gay. I was told to keep a distance from him during breaks..."

The conceit of Colman's fondly remembered series is that each episode is some celebrity's favorite story, and that fact is detailed in each show's opening. But the special status of the *Carol* is confirmed yet again, when Colman introduces it by stating that, "this week's *Favorite Story* is the choice of no *one* person, but of everyone in the English-speaking world..." Later in a somewhat less lofty vein, commerce is brought back into the equation a bit when announcer Joseph Kearn reminds the listeners that, "Ronald Colman recreates especially for *Favorite Story* listeners, the role... which he portrayed so memorably in a recent Decca album...." (Which—lo!—had just been reissued in the new 45 rpm format. A "plug," they call that now, and probably called it then.)

On Christmas Eve day of that same year of 1949, Edmund Gwenn returned to the role of Scrooge for a several-year run on *Stars Over Hollywood*, stepping into the slippers earlier worn there by Basil Rathbone.

Fresh from winning an Oscar (in the same year as fellow Scrooge Ronald Colman) for his work as Kris Kringle in 1947's *Miracle on 34th Street*, Gwenn's pivot from the second nicest Christmas icon to the nastiest is highlighted with relish by the announcer of the actor's 1951 *Stars* Scrooge. The show's short slot, and time lost to Intro, Commercials, Close, and framing device makes for a truncated *Carol*. But in those framing segments, Gwenn's warm, avuncular Kringle style is used to good effect when doubling as Charles Dickens, narrator of the story—and he seems to be having great fun when he turns to grumbling and rasping as the old miser!

That same framing device is also heard in the available 1951 and 1953 *Stars* Carols. In fact both use the exact same script, so the 1949 edition likely did as well. The texts for 1951 and 1953 are even identical as to the actor's "off the cuff" (!) banter with the announcer at the tail, which likely means this *Stars* script was standard to that series, at least throughout Gwenn's run with the piece.

Young Lonnie Burr would become one of Walt Disney's original Mousketeers in 1955—but in 1953, he was Edmund Gwenn's Tiny Tim:

"I believe I knew 'A Christmas Carol' by this time via films, the Brit version; I hadn't heard it on radio.

Where we did the show, I would guess CBS on Sunset. (Near NBC at Sunset and Vine, no longer extant, where we did *Dr. Paul*, a soap on which I was the child lead, 'Chris Martin.') Rehearsal was as usual: read through, hear SFX, notes from director then, you're on. The terse way of getting together, plus my age, did not leave much time for interaction and I was focused on my work, not hi-jinks and palaver. So frankly, I don't recall that much at all about the cast.

Except Parley Baer—he was pleasant to work with, as was Jack Kruschen and MOST of the cast; a few of the radio 'names' were not. (Much later, Parley and Jack read roles when I was the staff writer of over 20 scripts produced for radio's 'Heartbeat Theatre' from the Salvation Army in the '70s & '80s.)

Now, back then, as I mention in my memoir, it was a time when one was still allowed to imagine in a medium other than a book. In Films/TV—also in plays—you are SHOWN or TOLD what to concentrate on and precisely what things are, even if it is Sci-Fi. In Radio you are allowed the freedom that no other medium can match.

Some of my favorites were *Inner Sanctum* (I did a good, young version of the squeaky door opening); George & Gracie (who are in my comedy team book); *Amos & Andy* (also in my book—but don't tell anybody or I'll be accused of something or other!); *Fibber McGee and Molly* (book, too): and *The Jack Benny Show*.

Ostensibly, radio is lost now except for talking heads and 'music'. But over the years in addition to those "Heartbeats" over 500 stations, I also did some hour shows, cut versions of two of my plays, for American Radio Theatre. (All of my radio scripts, etc., are in the Lonnie Burr Collection in the Thousand Oaks Library in Southern California—by the way, one of the best and most prolific places in the country for radio recordings, history and so on.)

That is about all I can remember for certain about my 'Christmas Carol' (YOWZA!!!) Although it is a small role, I would like to hear what I sounded like at 9—there were NO comp copies in that time frame!"

Your author was able to remedy the problem of the missing aircheck for Mr. Burr nearly sixty years on. After which he responded:

"It is always a shock for a guy to hear how high and squeaky he sounded as a kid!"

Since that Tiny Tim/Mousketeer era, Lonnie has acted on TV, in film, and on stage, as well as writing in many media and working as a choreographer and a director. All this and more is detailed on his website, mouseketeerlonnieburr.com.

While we are discussing British-born Scrooge portrayers in America, we'll touch on some *Carol*s which originated on British airwaves that bounced to these shores as well:

In 1949, a syndicated Harry Alan Towers *Carol* featured a cast of renowned J. Arthur Rank Organization film actors. Led by John Mills as Scrooge, the cast included among others Margaret Lockwood,

Dirk Bogarde, Jean Simmons, Googie Withers, and Alec Guinness. Which leads us to—

—the 1951 American Broadcasting Company presentation of a BBC production in which Alec Guinness starred as Scrooge.

Guinness of course was one of that select group of legendary English actors who had long Twentieth Century careers that began on stage and eventually embraced all media—a storied group that included such fellow *Carol*ers as John Gielgud, Laurence Olivier, and Ralph Richardson. Guinness is known for many films including his early Ealing comedies, *The Bridge on the River Kwai*, the original *Tinker, Tailor, Soldier, Spy*, and of course *Star Wars*—though he did not like to be reminded of the career-obscuring latter role of Obi Wan Kenobi. He was often considered the best film actor of his aforementioned peers, and was no stranger to radio.

But his Ebenezer is a strangely low-energy one, more stuffy than edgy (interestingly, he would create a similarly odd Marley in the 1970 film musicalization of the story); and so like Reginald Owens's miser of 1938, it is an oddly lackluster Scrooge. The production too is a bit detached and schoolish; probably not surprising for one introduced with a sterile reading of the words, "The BBC presents a famous actor…in a famous story."

And the compression of the story is as flawed as that of several of the American streamliners. There are many good things missing: no scene between employer and employee at the end of the day, no Marley doorknocker, and not even a lead character onstage until Scrooge enters the office more than three minutes into a broadcast that only has twenty-eight in which to tell his story. Instead, after a faithfully Dickensian opening by the narrator (though unfortunately, this storyteller more reads than performs his text throughout), we are treated to a picturesque London street scene rather than to a brisk introduction of Ebenezer Scrooge and Bob Cratchit. Compounding these painful lacks, there are odd additions as well: Marley spells out who the other coming ghosts will be, robbing the story of an element of suspense, and the guests at Fezziwig's play Musical Chairs instead of dancing!

But the rich music score by Harold Evans is very good, and most of the acting is solid. In particular, we get a nice, fulsome Christmas

Present (though the dialogue he is given is clumsy and rushed, not even allowing the poor Ghost his touching transitional goodbye scene before Future appears.) And the scenes at Bob's and Fred's homes seem full of heart. But the climax is undercut, with no scene-setting sound effects at the cemetery and instead, stiff expository dialogue from poor Scrooge. This all leads us to a Christmas morning with a Turkey Boy who sounds to be about twenty years old, which makes the line "What—the one (turkey) as big as me?" laughable in the wrong way. And this "boy" just happens to know Bob Cratchit! Who just then shows up in Scrooge's bedroom to remind his boss of Fred's invitation to dinner! Whereupon his bosses' cheery welcoming inquiry to Bob about his beloved son Tim is (wait for it...)

"He's not *dead*, is he?" (!)

In short, yet again The Loekle Rule is proven in spades: there is no gain in attempting to gild a beautiful lily, especially when the "gold" you have in hand is actually brass.

Two years after this misfire, 1953 saw another transatlantic *Carol* as a part of *Theatre Royal* on NBC, with a similarly famous and gifted actor in the lead.

Sir Laurence Olivier was worthy of his reputation as one of the best English-language actors of his century. His work on stage, from London to Broadway, was legendary; and many of his films, from *Wuthering Heights* to *Richard III*, from *Marathon Man* to *The Entertainer*, are classics today. He left us with memorable versions of such iconic characters as Hamlet, Maxim de Winter, and even Zeus, but alas, unlike many of the other gifted actors we're covering in these pages, he came a cropper with Ebenezer Scrooge.

As with Orson Welles in 1938, the Ebenezer there is a broadly played, stereotypical "Old Man." And worse, Olivier's fellow actors do lackluster work as well in a flat, under-produced Harry Alan Towers program that is saddled with a pedestrian script. Yet another adaptation that substitutes words of coal for Dickens' gems (do you see a pattern here, dear reader?), and which adds insult to that injury by telling the story through narration, more than by enacting it with dialogue.

But there were always plenty of new opportunities to get the story right!

Even as the high-profile shows we've discussed continued to be produced during the "Golden Age of (Network) Radio," right down through the years since it all began at WEAF New York on Christmas Eve of 1922, many was the "other good old city, town, or borough" that continued to sing its own local *Carol*.

True, some broadcasts involved network Radio *Carol* Stock Company persona, such as the one from WOR New York and WOL, Washington, D.C. in 1944 with Ernest Chappell and Everett Sloane. But many were wholly local, such as the one from WRNL Richmond in 1939, the one from WGES Chicago in 1942 in Lithuanian (!), and one from ye author's own childhood listening area, CKLW Detroit's in 1953. That production was even lauded by no less a national showbiz arbiter than *Variety*:

> "Biggest production in (the station's) history proved... sock entertainment.... Modernized version of (Carol) used 55 persons... (and the) entire show flowed smoothly.... Commercial spiel, harmonious with season and program, was choice."

The showbiz rag had similar fulsome praise for that same Christmas' *Carol* from WCFM in Washington, D.C.:

> "Crowded by major web holiday programs and big name shows, this local effort was significant for its success as a moving, polished production and as an example of an attention-getting labor of love on a local level."

It sounds like a few of these supposed "lightweight" local contenders may actually have bested some of the heavyweights we have covered. (For many, many more of these "Little *Carol*s That Could," see the Log at the back of this book.)

And even these are not all...

For while all of these actors, national and local, renowned and unrenowned, were treading the boards of the ether in at the same time as Lionel Barrymore, the *Carol* was conquering yet another closely related medium.

STAVE 5:
Costing but a few Pounds of your Mortal Money

"There would be a moment of silence before the needle was dropped, and we'd all hold our breath—then, that familiar scratchy sound under the Hammond Organ riff, as the curtain rose once more on the story of Scrooge: 'MARLEY was dead, to begin with...!'"

—Julie Ashton

During the same era when radio ruled the airwaves, the classic story was also recorded directly for home-use on 78 rpm discs. They were generally produced in the then-current radio style, often by radio personnel and with radio casts. And The Master's story was as powerful when arising from shellac or vinyl as when broadcast—if not more so, due to the "this is a special presentation just for those of us gathered in this room" characteristic of the medium. As listener Julie Ashton recalls:

> "We were a Navy family, so the sites of the Christmas Eves of my childhood ranged from the early 50s in a tropical Philippine home, to a Colorado Springs ranch house, and then the barracks quarters on the South Boston Shipyard. But our favorite tradition always traveled with us....
>
> We would turn off all but the Christmas tree lights while Dad lit the fire in the fireplace, and my sister, my two brothers, and I would all settle in to listen to the old 78 rpm record set of Ernest Chappell's 'A Christmas Carol.' ...The old-fashioned radio play organ was unparalleled in its power to evoke emotion and excitement, and each silent, careful change of records would replay in our minds our favorite scenes:
>
> Christmas Present with its gorgeous color...
>
> Scrooge in his terror at the gravesite...
>
> Scrooge in his conversion, flinging open his bedroom window: 'I haven't missed it! Oh, thank you, spirits!'
>
> In my memory, these scenes would play throughout the year. Years later as a professional singer, I played the young Belle in a musical version. But my heart was still with our Chappell production and this 'new'

version fell flat—the particular cast of Chappell's recording will always be the definitive voices of Dickens' Carol for me! And to this day, Dickens is my favorite writer, and his words still amaze and inspire.

But with the years, the records got ever scratchier, and by the late 60s were unplayable. I somehow hung on to the set through the first years of marriage, but finally discarded them.

Then, after seven years of searching each Christmas (I had no idea so many versions were out there!), a Google for the image of the green, red, and white Victorian cover illustration finally yielded results! I would never have imagined when we listened years before that future technology would so magically bring this beautiful memory back into my life, and into that of my brothers and my sister.

And into the lives of our own children!

God bless us, everyone!"

Of course previous decades had seen the *Carol* snippets recorded by Bransby Williams, Albert Whelan, William Sterling Battis, and others; but the Victor Records set that Julie recalls so fondly is one of the first such "long-form" home-record productions. It features another return to the Dickens fold by Ernest Chappell, of whom Arthur Anderson recalls, "I had a great respect for him. He was one of the top radio announcers."

And from the writer/producer/narrator's remarks in the liner notes, we can see that he took the task seriously. After quoting Dickens' Forward from the original book (it seems few Carolers can resist doing that), Chappell writes:

Announcer and actor Ernest Chappell of *Quiet Please*, *The Campbell Playhouse*, and several radio and audio *Carol*s.

"Within the confines of (this album's) forty minutes it is the hope of the adapter that you who treasure 'A Christmas Carol' will find most of your favorite scenes... Would that we could tell the tale in full, unhindered by the necessary mechanics which confound all methods of tale-telling."

(Of course later technological advances in recording would bring his wish to pass, with ever-fuller, and eventually even *complete*, recordings of Dickens' text.)

> "And be assured of this, you lovers of Dickens' works, we have not trifled with the telling. Too often in contemporary adapting, liberties are taken with traditional writings. Throughout our preparation we have been mindful of the values you may hold in each scene, each line, even in a word…(this is) as Dickens' set it down and we'd not change it."

(Chappell was evidently familiar with the failings of some previous audio productions of the story, perhaps even the benighted 1933 adaptation reviled earlier in these pages.)

> "To you who know 'A Christmas Carol,' may this album arouse a pleasant nostalgia for Christmases past. To you who hear it for the first time, may it bring to your Christmas an even fuller measure of the Spirit of Christmas."

Julie Ashton, and a long list of listeners before and since including the present author, would say that Chappell succeeded admirably in that goal. His professed love for the piece shines through, and within the constraints of its forty-minute length, it is one of the most faithful *Carol*s in the medium. As contemporary reviewer Jay Walz wrote in *The Washington Post*:

> "It is all done with the utmost sympathy for the Christmas spirit, with the appropriate exception of the part of Scrooge who is played most villainously by Eustace Wyatt."

And an old, cranky, very British Scrooge is indeed well played by Wyatt. Of whom, says Arthur Anderson:

> "Eustace Wyatt was a profane, hearty, slightly Cockney actor who was a totally different personality from the others (in the Mercury company.) He and a partner ran a pet shop in New York which sold, I believe, goldfish!"

And others in Chappell's hand-picked seasoned cast included Richard Gordon (radio's early Sherlock Holmes and 1931 Scrooge), Bud Collyer (radio's Superman), Leslie Woods, Alfred Shirley, and Larry Robinson (late beloved Friends of Old Time Radio performer.) And as "Master Peter Cratchit," there was one "Master Dickie Van Patten," who recalls:

> "I was about 12 years old when I played in that record, which was done in New York on the third floor of NBC. I'm not sure how I got the job—I was a kid, you know!—but I know I had already been doing *Let's Pretend*.
>
> I had never heard the story done on the radio.
>
> (But I used to listen to the radio—I used to listen to Uncle Don. That was a very popular kid's show, it was on like at 5:00 at night. You know the story of what happened to Uncle Don: he said, 'Good night, Kiddies. See you tomorrow.' And then he said (he didn't know the mike was still on), 'That'll settle the little sons of b&#*hes!' That was the end of Uncle Don!)
>
> As far as the cast, I knew Larry Robinson (Tiny Tim) really well—he had been my understudy in the play *On Borrowed Time*.

(A classic boy's role that both young actors also shared with Stuffy Singer.)

"He was very good and very good looking (as a kid, anyway!) And I remember Leslie Woods (Belle), and I knew Bud Collyer (Fred) well.

I was excited about doing *A Christmas Carol*, because I already knew the story—my father had read it to me."

Dick Van Patten is probably best remembered today as the father on the 1970s TV series *Eight is Enough*. He worked very extensively in that medium, beginning with a long run as a son in the early family series *Mama* (aka *I Remember Mama*.). His radio work in addition to *Let's Pretend* included a regular role on *Duffy's Tavern*, and a turn as Ethel Barrymore's son on *Miss Hattie*. He has also appeared on Broadway, and at New York City Opera in Rodgers and Hammerstein's *Cinderella*. (In a cast that included his fellow *Carol*er Bernadette Fiorella, the wife of the present author—who she in turn also shares *Carol*dom with. There are often even less than "six degrees of separation" in the wide world of Scrooge & co.!)

Of course, all for-home-use records like the one Patten appeared on carried a standard "Not Licensed for Broadcast" warning—but anecdotal evidence tells us that local radio stations were not above ignoring it. Richard Carlson of the jazzoLOG website tells us his opinion of the Chappell production, and how it was used in a novel way back then by his father, J. Ralph Carlson:

"Dad went into local theater and radio. He used to play Santa Claus at the biggest on-air celebration of the holiday in our hometown of Jamestown, New York. But there was another side to my father...and he found a way to celebrate that on Christmas too. Beginning sometime in the late 1940s, Dad devised a one-man radio production of Dickens' 'A Christmas Carol.'

At first there may have been a handful of other actors, and of course the ever-present

Hammond organ accompaniment of George Pfleeger in all his original work. Eventually an electric transcription (ET) was made of the show which was played thereafter every year, but before that it was done live—and I have memories of watching these programs from a space reserved for me under the studio piano. In fact, one year I even was given a line to say—no, not Tiny Tim. I got to be the boy Scrooge calls to Christmas morning about the turkey hanging in the butcher's window. I got to shout, from under the piano, 'It's hangin' there STILL!'

But soon my father figured out a way to do it all, narrating and playing Scrooge—and in a format that took only around half an hour. The other voices had been recorded painstakingly by one of the two brilliant engineers we had working at WJTN. His name was Ray Frehm, and he'd try to do anything you asked him—a rare trait in a radio engineer. My father had discovered the production on 12" 78 RPM RCA Victor records, done by a cast headed by Eustace Wyatt and a collection of the most familiar voices in radio drama of that day. Radio did not fool around, these people were contracted actors, and the images they created in imaginations of those who heard them have lasted a lifetime. This production of 'A Christmas Carol' was like that, and my father loved it. I did too, and to this day it is my favorite acted version—bar none.

Now what my father did was he got Ray to record, possibly first on wire recording (an almost impossible medium, because if it broke it was like a spring that flew into a snarling mess all over the studio) and later on tape, specific speeches which he lifted off the 78s. My father would signal or 'throw a cue' from the studio to Ray to start and stop the tape for a flowing dialogue. By 1950 or so, I think, the stolen speeches had been honed to perfection and cut onto an ET for easier handling in the control room.

My father and the station did not think they were stealing. After all, commercial records got played on the radio everyday, and this was a commercial release. Artists got paid, in a very circuitous fashion, by the stations and the networks

For years, I listened to those 78s all the time—and still probably can recite most of it from memory. Mr. Wyatt's Scrooge was heartchilling, as was my father's and all the truly great ones. There is no sign of redemption in the character—he barks, he threatens, he taunts. The challenge for all actors who attempt creation of this role is the graveyard scene when Scrooge begs for mercy. (I thought my father's delivery became too shrill—but he was soaked with sweat when he finished each year.)

My father became known for both his Santa and his Scrooge around our town—and so Christmas each year absolutely sparkled beyond belief! J. Ralph had a daily radio program of common sense inspiration, which he called 'The Radio Scrapbook.' George accompanied in flawless improvisation at the electric organ. It probably was pretty corny, but the town

Cheery custom *Carol* creator J. Ralph Carlson at the WJTN mike. (Courtesy of Richard Carlson.)

and especially my mother loved it.

He honored Tiny Tim and Dickens in each show with his closing salutation—which now I will leave with you: 'God bless us... every one.'

Around this same time, the present author's hometown station of WONW in Defiance, Ohio presented a two-day *Christmas with the Stars* extravaganza. "With the Stars" on the air, yes—but was this done with the Stars' permission? Both Ronald Colman and Lionel Barrymore's *Carol*s were a part of the programming, as well as Charles Laughton's *Mr. Pickwick's Christmas*, Loretta Young's *The Littlest Angel*, Bing Crosby's *The Small One*, and several other audio Christmas classics. All were presented in twenty-to-twenty five minute chunks that conveniently left room for sponsors' commercials in each thirty minute slot, and all just happen to have been previously released on 78 rpm records.

Hmmm...

Actually, in local markets far from the prying eyes of record company lawyers, where broadcasts like these were as ephemeral as Dickens's Ghosts, with no evidence of them lasting past the Yuletide, such practices were probably common.

That same December 1941 of Chappell's record *Carol* was the infamous season of Pearl Harbor; and America needed all the Christmas cheer it could muster. Another new *Carol* album was in the stores then as well, destined to become perhaps the most famous in this format.

That twenty-five minute Decca Records dramatization starred Ronald Colman as Scrooge, who also narrates the story. He's supported by such radio stalwarts as Barbara Jean Wong, Gale Gordon (of TV's *Lucy Show*) as Christmas Future (yes, again, a spoken role), and Hans Conried, of whom a fellow Caroler who we'll hear from shortly, Tommy Cook, says, "Hans was brilliant—I have great memories of working with him."

The script by George Wells is the same one later used for the Colman radio production mentioned in the previous chapter. And though serviceable enough as radio/audio writing, it is yet another dramatization that sacrifices many of Dickens' own fit phrases for an adapter's less effective ones. Add to this such plot choices such as the "un-muting" of the last Ghost, and the odd twist upon Dickens' climax whereby it is at TINY TIM's gravesite that Scrooge repents rather than his own (!), and we have still more proof if needed that concerns about violating Dickens text went unheard, or were unheeded, by many writers.

Interior art from Ronald Colman's 78 rpm *Carol* album, featuring John Leech's illustrations from the book's first edition.

(Collector's Corner, 1941 edition: several later LP reissues of this production omit the charity collectors scene, which is still unrestored on the current commercially available CD.)

The next year's disc offering was from Columbia Records. It employs a text by Edith Meiser that has the same fault as Colman's—too many of the current writer's own words, and too few of Dickens'. Radio historian William Nadel knew the writer well, and states that the script was essentially the same as the one used for her 1931 NBC *Carol* in the *Sherlock Holmes* time slot. And in another bit of synergy, the 1942 album's production was directed by Edith's ex-husband, Tom McKnight, who was then working on the current *Holmes* series.

But aside from script issues, the music by Leith Stevens is solid, and Basil Rathbone is very good in the lead (which as mentioned earlier, he would play several times more on both radio and television.) "C.C." in a contemporary *Classical Recordings* review wrote:

> "Basil Rathbone is the newest in a long and honorable line who turn from crusty skinflint to Lord Bountiful at the annual behest of record companies intent of reaping the holiday harvest with Dickens' 'Christmas Carol.' The elegant and expert English actor turns in a crack job by avoiding the more lachrymose quagmires, and by creating a dimensional characterization with voice alone. The adaptation…is by Edith Meiser, who once was a monologist worth hearing…and that familiar voice of Christmas Past belongs to Francis X. Bushman."

Just nearing the age of sixty as this album was released, Bushman had been a matinee idol on the stage and in silent film, including playing the heavy Messala in the original *Ben-Hur*. Also a veteran mike actor by this point in his long career, he is joined in this *Carol* by a sterling radio cast: Lurene Tuttle, Arthur Q. Bryan, Elliot Lewis, Walter Tetley, narrator Harlow Wilcox, and Tommy Cook. We'll hear more from Tommy in a moment, but first a recollection from listener Jane Blalock:

> "Our original album of this was bought by my Dad, probably in 1950 or 1951. The first year I remember listening to it, I was 3 years old…. It had been a snowy week in Tulsa, OK, and just days before, we had moved to another house. There were no curtains yet, and we sat in the front room, I on my Dad's lap, and listened to this story with the lights out. It was full of voices, and sound effects: walking on wood floors, chains, thumps,

doors opening/closing, sleigh bells; and singing, narration, theme and background music indicating change of scenes, etc.... It was a very exciting and slightly "creepy" tale—and I loved it! Thereafter, including other younger siblings as they came along, this became our tradition every Christmas Eve before we went to bed—sometimes in candle light or total darkness as we grew older.

The year my own 3rd child was born, my mother brought me a cassette copy which thereafter became OUR new family's tradition until the tape was lost in a move. I looked for any kind of copy on the Internet for a long time, and one day found a Basil Rathbone website where I posted. Around 2005, I received a treasure: a brand new CD of the exact recording, complete with familiar artwork on the front label. It is once again our family tradition, after close to 60 years—and now with grandkids!

The story is amazingly complete, very full and easy to follow; the British dialogue is crisp and very clear. It is the kind of recording guaranteed to excite the imagination of any child, and certainly hold the interest of every adult."

The liner notes for the production so dear to Jane's heart tell us that Tommy Cook played both "Young Scrooge, (and) the child who converted (Scrooge)—Tiny Tim." The present author has had the very real pleasure of acting at the mike with Tommy at the Friends of Old Time Radio Conventions. He is as talented as ever, with a vibrant voice that belies the age of a man who has had such a lengthy career, and he recalls:

Basil "Scrooge" Rathbone with Tommy "Tiny Tim" Cook in his arms. Though undated, this picture with Greer Garson, Bobby Winkler, and cast appears to be from a broadcast of *Goodbye, Mr. Chips* a few months before the 1942 *Carol* recording session. (Courtesy of Tommy Cook.)

"Arch Oboler had discovered me in '38 or '39. They used to have a radio artist's bureau at NBC—Fay Reagan—and they took out an article in one of the magazines that said 'free auditions.' So my mother took me there. (You know, there was nothing worse than a stage mother! A bad one, they were vicious. But my mother was one of the real good ones. And she kept beautiful scrapbooks for all the shows in my early years; and the actors I worked with would, you know, they'd add a comment or two.)

So to cut to the chase, I auditioned. I had the youngest sounding voice, and I got the role in Arch Oboler's 'Every Man's Theater.' (I ended up over the years starring in five or six award-winning shows for him.) That first one was starring Alla Nazimova, and somehow I played a little German kid! I don't know where I got the accent—I was so young! But somehow, I was able to do it.

When I did this 'Christmas Carol,' I was about eleven at the time—I'll be eighty-two soon!—and I didn't really know the story, just remnants (too busy I guess, just being a kid and getting into trouble!) The one thing that is important to me, is that the top radio actors were absolutely brilliant! Some notes on the ones in this show:

Eliott Lewis (Fred) was probably the best actor during radio's Golden Years; he could play any role. He later wrote and directed the 'Sears Radio Theater' with Fletcher Markle (I starred on several of those). Jay Novello (Bob Cratchit) was a fine character actor—worked with him so often. Francis X. Bushman (Christmas Past), a distinguished film actor, appeared with me often on the radio *Red Ryder*. Rhoda Williams (Fan) and I did so many shows together as child actors. Paula Winslowe (Mrs. Cratchit) played my mother on *The Life of Riley*—she was wonderful. Walter Tetley (Turkey Boy) from *The Great Gildersleeve* series was so talented, but had some kind of strange aging condition that kept his voice young. And Harlow Wilcox was one of the distinguished announcers, and nice to work with. Dix Davis (Peter)—brilliant—was the best all-around child actor from the West Coast. He was Pinky on *One Man's Family*, and starred opposite Louise Erickson in *A Date With Judy*, directed by Helen Mack—I replaced Dix when he left the show. (Now, I think I was truly the best child DRAMATIC radio actor, going beyond just acting and reading lines to somehow naturally becoming that young character, baring my soul and personality, and thus connecting with the listening audience.)"

(Readers will note that several of the actors mentioned here—Rathbone, Davis, and Bryan—were, or would become, repeat *Carol*ers.)

"You know, I was the original Little Beaver in the *Red Ryder* movie serial, I starred in six independent films and won the Photoplay Award, and I did God knows how many television shows—but the greatest people I ever worked with were in radio! Laymen probably think, 'Well, it's easy. Somebody gets on and reads from a script.'"

(Sadly, some people on both sides of the mike still think that. And Tommy's right—they're wrong.)

"But no—it's talent. And the top actors never really woodshedded. They understood the characters and then just laid their souls out when it got on the radio waves, you know?

Radio was supreme. The three greatest in the halcyon days of radio as far as writer-producer-directors were Oboler, Norman Corwin, and Orson Welles. And those three always could get any major star in a film to be on their shows—everyone! They would just, you know, give a call and say, 'I've got a show. I'd like you to be on.' And James Stewart or whoever it was would say, 'Sure, love to do it.'

I don't recall much more about *A Christmas Carol* (though I think I may actually have done it more than once?) But I do I have a picture in my files by a network photog where I'm being held up in the arms of Basil Rathbone, because I'm such a little squirt!"

(And since the 1940s?)

"Well, there were other actors, and finally I just outgrew the roles and went on....

But as far as voice, I still do SPERDVAC (you know, a radio convention here in LA), and REPS in Seattle—they still invite me. And it was wonderful in the last year or so, because I starred in shows written by Arch Oboler who discovered me back in '38 or '39! Also, I'm the voice of the International Tennis Hall of Fame. Tennis has been a big part of my life. I was a Southern California Junior Champion, I produce Celebrity Charity Tennis, Gold, and Skiing Events all over the world, and I wrote a tennis screenplay. So it's been an honor for me to do the voiceovers for all the Grand Slam events.

I'm actually behind the camera now—I've created a couple of pictures, a television series, a new reality show, and my son and I are working on a combination talk/interview/comedy/music game show.

And you know, I'm on the Board of Pacific Pioneer Broadcasters. And back then, those were wonderful actors, and the nicest people—and the greatest memories I've ever had. Wonderful radio days."

That seems to be the consensus, Mr. Cook—both from the creators, and from the listeners.

But now back to radio's sister medium, records:

As mentioned in the previous chapter, MGM Records offered their own home edition Lionel Barrymore *Carol* in 1947. In an article from *The Tuscaloosa News* syndicated when that production was aired by CBS in 1957, veteran producer, director and writer Dailey Paskman asserts that he had been associated with the actor on most Barrymore broadcasts of the Dickens tale. The present author has not found documentation for that claim, and it does seem doubtful in the case of collaborators like Orson Welles and his Campbell's writer, Howard Koch. But Paskman was a seasoned show business creative talent, with radio credits dating back to the early 1920's; and he did in fact later publish his own musical adaptation of the tale, *Scrooge*, so he may indeed have a hand in several of Barrymore's productions.

The producer states that during the period when he was working with the man he called "Dear Scrooge" on other record projects, he persuaded Barrymore to record his characterization for posterity. (Broadcast transcriptions were not then considered in the same light as records produced in the studio for home sale, and in cases where they even existed, were often unavailable because of rights issues.)

Paskman says that they adapted several versions of Dickens' story before finding one that completely satisfied Barrymore, and that

> April 26th, 1946
>
> To Dr. Eugene Zador
>
> Dailey Paskman was successful in consumating a contract with ARA, Inc. for an additional five(5%)percent payment over the regular standard royalty fee for records.
>
> Of the above mentioned five(5%)percent item we will divide money payments into three equal parts - one(1/3)third for each of us: Barrymore - Paskman - Zador. This will allow payment to you for reducing orchestration combination, and for preparing and coaching vocalists for the recording session scheduled for May 1st, 1946, with Mr. Paskman as executive producer.
>
> *Lionel Barrymore*
>
> *Dailey Paskman*

Letter of agreement concerning one of Dailey Paskman and Lionel Barrymore's several record projects, addressed to the actor's music composition instructor. (Courtesy of Historyforsale.com.)

the star insisted on employing only English actors for this production. (As with his claim to have worked on most of Lionel's radio *Carol*s, there may be a bit of benign exaggeration in that statement—Barrymore himself is of course American, narrator Richard Hale hailed from Tennessee, and the Turkey Boy of this recording sounds Yankee-raised to this auditor.)

Paskman reports that when Barrymore heard the final version he remarked:

"I wanted to do the best one I've ever done…and I hope this one will be heard for as many years as there are Christmases to come."

And among Lionel's many *Carol*s, it ranks well. Though his voice is thickened a bit by age by this time in his life, he brings his best game—his dismissals of Fred in the opening scene build beautifully to a drippingly disdainful and acidly comic, "…*Get OUUUUUUT*!!!" And the solid script shows the effort the two men put into it, with well-formed scenes and able descriptions. It generously grants almost a full minute of the only twenty-four available to set the opening scene, and the storytelling there and throughout by Hale is strong. (Film fans may recall the sharp-featured actor's striking performance as Boo Radley's father in *To Kill A Mockingbird*.)

Veteran television and film actor Michael C. Gwynne remembers:

> "Barrymore, in the version in the 78 rpm album, was the guy for me. My brother and I, he two years younger, were left alone a lot, and found no trouble in this as we were brought up to be self-sufficient first and to ask questions later. My father's first words that I remember were an argument of sorts, where my mother was telling me that my crayon coloring book I was working on had trees and that the trees were supposed to be green (I guess I was using another color.) I heard my Dad say, 'Let him do it.'
>
> That was it for me from then on I suppose…
>
> Anyway, we had a huge floor model radio that told us stories, but that also had a lift-off top that held that miracle of miracles—a turntable with auto changing mechanism. Underneath, a small library of 78 rpm albums: Bozo adventures, some jazz sides including Woody Herman's *Bijou* (which I can still whistle and

Lionel Barrymore's Scrooge with Dickie Hall's Tiny Tim in the 1944 *Life* magazine photo that inspired the cover art for the actor's 1947 *Carol* record set. (For that full-color painting, see back cover of this book.)

hum to this day), along with a jumpy little number called *The Four Brothers*.

But the gem, the treasure, was *A Christmas*

Carol with Lionel Barrymore!!! Painted on the cover with a child on his lap that I used to imagine was me...but that now seeing the braced leg, I know to be Tiny Tim!"

"Even at 6 years of age I knew how to run that turntable and play those babies whenever the folks were out dancing or whatever. My brother would be asleep, and I would play DJ.

(Man, oh man, and how prescient *that* was to be...)

I can still hear 'Uncle Lionel,' (as John Barrymore Jr. used to call him whenever we'd be drinking together back in my Hollywood days) intoning those immortal lines with that great music in the background. I found the production online some years ago, but it was never quite the same as sliding those heavy 78s on the turntable, switching those plastic knobs, and adjusting the volume to come out of the cloth-covered venerable old RCA piece of magical furniture.

As I lay there on the floor, I knew I was in for a first class journey—and I was usually found sleeping on that rug when the folks got home.

My first doorway to the outside world. (*Sigh*.)"

As to Michael's comment that his playing these discs as a child was prescient: he would grow up to become a veteran of America radio's SECOND "golden age," as a 1960's Rock & Roll DJ.

And by way of these records, Michael's parents not only gave joy to their young son, but to an old trouper as well. From Lionel Barrymore's autobiography:

> "From time to time, in pursuit of Euterpe and money, I have made recordings involving music.... (One was) a composition of mine called Hallowe'en.... This and other narrations with music, such as A Christmas Carol and Rip Van Winkle, have been caught on wax. If you are full of curiosity and reckless with your money you can buy them in stores, and I hope you do. I get a small percentage."

They DID buy your *Carol* discs, Lionel—and those of many others as well.

For starting in this era, the record producers evidently got wind of the fact that there were many potential *Carol* listeners of young master Gwynne's age, because they began to produce versions specifically aimed at the moppet set.

The first seems to have been from Regal Record Corp in 1949, in their "Tots 'N' Teens" line of seven-inch kiddie 78 rpms. The disc held a just-over-three-minute telling of the *Carol* by Ireene Wicker, "The Singing Lady."

Taking into account the miniscule running time (and this *Carol* would have competition in that area), Wicker does a good job. The moral is there, the music is supportive, and her infectious voicing of the different characters shows why children loved her. Arthur Anderson, a radio listener long before he became a radio actor at the grand old age of eleven, says, "I didn't know about those records—but I sure listened to her on the radio!"

And these little bits of shellac where only the tip of a growing iceberg. As Richard Kleiner wrote in 1952 in a piece that appeared in the Henderson, N.C. *Times*:

> "*Kiddie Records No Child's Play In Money, Say Experts—Top Entertainers Clamor For Slice Of $15 Million Melon.*

(Courtesy of "Ernie [Not Bert] Blogspot")

> Children's records aren't child's play any more [sic]. There's big money in what *Variety*, the show business trade paper, calls 'kidisks'...."

(Ah, that pungent *Variety* lingo again!)

> "More and more children's records are featuring big-name artists...they can hear...Charles Laughton or Basil Rathbone or Ronald Colman tell 'A Christmas Carol'.... And the life expectancy of a good children's record is fabulously long....
>
> But...children have pretty emphatic opinions

> about what they like and don't like. 'Kids can spot phonies,' says the head of Columbia's children's record department, Hecky Krasno. 'They don't like people talking down to them.' So children's records have to be planned psychologically. To be successful, it takes, as RCA's Steve Carlin says, 'a combination of the right artist with the right material.' (And) only a few years ago a children's record consisted of (just) a piano and a man telling a story...."

(That being much the style of Ireene Wicker's production.)

> "More recently, record companies have taken greater pains with production.... But on the song and story records, the names are used to sell adults, not children. As one record official puts it 'Kids know from nothing about names, but Aunt Agatha buys somebody she's heard of.'"

And Auntie had surely heard of several of the seasoned actors who joined the "Dickens for the little dickens" sweepstakes during this era.

To start with, the Charles Laughton *Carol* cited in the article hit the stores in 1951.

Considered by many to be one of the most gifted actors of his time, Laughton began his career on the British and Broadway stage, but is best remembered for his excellent work in many classic films including his Oscar-winning *The Private Life of Henry VIII*, *Mutiny on the Bounty*, and the 1939 *Hunchback of Notre Dame*.

And from early in his career, he was also known as an accomplished public reader—much like the author of our subject tale, Mr. Dickens. In fact, among such things as an acclaimed stage reading of Shaw's *Don Juan in Hell* with fellow *Carol*er Agnes Moorehead and recorded passages from the Bible and Shakespeare, Laughton also did a recording where he read some Christmas portions of Dickens' *Pickwick Papers* which was double-billed with Ronald

Colman's *Carol* when it was reissued on LP.

In that same vein, the actor does not portray Scrooge in his *Carol*; like Lionel Barrymore in his 1938 radio performance, he serves as Narrator of the story. The editing is nicely done, and gives Laughton nearly five times as long as Wicker had to tell the tale—though at fifteen minutes, his storytelling manner is still a bit breathlessly paced.

Though their roles are small, the star is well supported by several other actors, including radio (and TV's *Outer Limits*) actor Vic Perrin as Marley's Ghost. This warm-hearted production likely worked very well for the little listeners seated on the rug around their portable record players. And it may have been broadcast as well at some point, for though first released on home-use 78 rpms, it has also been seen as a white-label 33 1/3 LP in DJ/Demo format.

Not long after this one from RCA Victor, another celebrity brought forth a *Carol*ette from Cricket Records. Though not the stage and screen luminary that Laughton was, Brett Morrison was very much a broadcasting star, with a long and varied career that ranged from soap opera (*Stella Dallas*) to the Bible (*Light of the World*). But he is best known for his role as The Shadow—in fact, many aficionados rate his Lamont Cranston higher than that of one-time Scrooge Orson Welles. And Morrison would stay with the audio medium until the very end.... He recreated his most famous role in new LP adventures in the 1960s, and had just finished an episode of *Heartbeat Theatre* (see Lonnie Burr's comments in the previous chapter) when he was stricken by a coronary in 1978.

Now, the mythical "Aunt Agatha" mentioned in the article above may have been fond of the two stars we've just mentioned. But in the eyes of the Fifties kids themselves, the next one probably easily trumped them both!

1955 saw Golden Records, a relatively young label that was rising to real prominence in the children's records niche, release *Howdy Doody—Charles Dickens' A Christmas Carol*. It starred that genuine superstar of the new Kid's TV world, Howdy Doody (yes, the marionette cowboy voiced by Buffalo Bob Smith) as Bob Cratchit, with fellow Doodyville denizens Captain Scuttlebutt (probably voiced by Allen Swift) as Scrooge, and Dilly Dally (likely voiced by

Billy LeCornec) as Tiny Tim. A semi-musicalized three minutes with chorus, it is harmless enough, if a bit "cartoonier" than The Singing Lady's similar short rendition of the story.

Perhaps what made the record companies think that these short-short *Carols* were even feasible was the kind of "mental expansion" that is asked today of TV commercial watchers: a spot debuts in its original long form of sixty seconds, but over the duration of its air run, the sponsor saves money by later only paying to air a thirty-second cut of it, and sometimes at last, even a fifteen-second one, knowing that the repeat viewer's mind fills in the blanks of what's missing. Perhaps the *Carol* had so seeped into the public consciousness by way of a century of books, plays, films, and broadcasts that a highlights version would suffice to get its whole point across. This may be the explanation, too, for Barrymore's comment about how audiences didn't seem to notice the script changes in his various versions over the years—they were replaying their old experiences of the story over in their minds simultaneously with each of his new performances of it.

Next up on the record changer (for those who remember such a mechanism):

Just as the decade changed over to the 1960s, Laughton, Colman, and Rathbone's fellow expat Brit Hollywood star Claude Rains took what appears to have been his only turn at bat as the old skinflint.

Rains' father was an actor, and young Claude made his stage debut at age eleven. He served in World War I in the same London Scottish Regiment as fellow future *Carol*ers Basil Rathbone and Ronald Colman, and then returned to the British stage. He was an acting instructor as well, numbering among his students two more illustrious Carolers-to-be, Laurence Olivier and John Gielgud. Rains would go on to a stellar career in film, from Capra's *Mr. Smith Goes to Washington*, to *Casablanca*, to Lean's *Lawrence of Arabia*, but his first film would always remain one of his most famous; and like the record we speak of, 1933's *The Invisible Man* was (largely) a vocal performance.

His *Carol* from Mercury/Childcraft uses a variation of Colman's narrative device: Scrooge himself tells the tale; or rather here, he and his conscience, who pitches in by way of a filtered mike.

The duration of this single is a bit longer than either Wicker's or Doody's; and those two were a bit more juvenile in the first case, and cartoonish in the latter. But strangely enough, they both succeed better on their own terms.

For at just five and a half minutes, and with the piece essentially just one long descriptive monologue by Rains with no real character interaction (the only other voices are in snatches of choral singing), it is neither long enough nor variegated enough to really succeed in its goal as a semi-straight telling of the whole story. But we'll give it an "A for effort" for even undertaking such an impossible task. (The early audio shorts by performers including Williams, Whelan, and Battis don't count in this competition, as they were intentionally excerpts, rather than attempts to cover the whole story.)

The passing years saw another short musicalization of the *Carol*, this one from James Kenny on Golden Records. And there were at

The Peter Pan Players' *Carol* has been heard by way of cassette, LP, and 45 rpm.

least two other multi-cast productions for children, one from Golden/Wonderland, and one from a major competitor in the field, Peter Pan Records—featuring respectively, as one might guess, The Wonderland Players and The Peter Pan Players (and Chorus).

"Oh, Backus, you've done it again!" There have been two separate Magoo Carols—the TV cartoon, and the later non-musical record.

Wonderland also released a record/book *Carol* of the "*beep—turn the page!*" variety, theirs featuring Mr. Magoo. It is not taken from the soundtrack of his classic animated TV version, but was obviously inspired by it. It even uses the same theatrical framing device: the narrator announces at the end that, "…and as the curtain came down…Mr. Magoo went home to rest up, because he had to do it all over again the next night…!" The production is an odd little duck featuring Tom Cipolla and an anonymous female voicer, but with star Jim Backus's lines obviously recorded independently of the other actors.

And speaking of *Carols* tied to the world of cartoons…

In 1975, a children's *Carol* was actually heard to come from the Magic Kingdom itself! And that production from Disneyland Records is rare in several ways:

It is one of the first instances of a large number of Disney's star characters appearing in the same story. And it is a reversal of the usual order of things in that this record would later be the basis for a film, 1983's animated featurette *Mickey's Christmas Carol*—which would in turn spawn its own soundtrack record.

And there was evidently a rare earlier variant version of this LP project with differences in album art, characters, and performers, including actor Bill Lee in the role of Scrooge. But when it did not perform well, veteran actor Alan Young (famous for the 1960's sitcom *Mr. Ed*) revitalized the project. With input from fellow voicer Alan Dinehart, he fashioned a new script—and being past member of a Dickens society, he did it very well indeed. (With perhaps one misstep: As in many dramatizations, there's an invented scene where Scrooge visits the Cratchits on Christmas Day, and of course by then he's become a very cheery chap. But after that, when the story still gives us the scene *next* morning where Bob comes into the office late and Ebenezer tries to act "Scrooge-y" again, we may for once credit Bob's fears that the poor old fellow truly is insane.)

But within the framework of the necessary trimming, streamlining, and simpler description called for by for a children's record, the production is pretty faithful to its source. And Young may have been familiar with the Colman versions, as his Scrooge also narrates the story in the past tense.

The added humor generally works well. When Cratchit (Mickey Mouse) seeks to add more coal to the fire to make the office warmer, Scrooge barks, "What are ye tryin' ta do, raise tomatoes?" And we learn that Mrs. Cratchit's pot on the stove is filled with Scrooge's laundry, to earn the family a few more pence. The songs and music are pleasant, and the sound effects work solid.

Young is very good as the old skinflint—who here of course, is Scrooge MCDUCK, the brilliant previous creation of legendary cartoonist Carl Barks. Born in England, Young had spent time in Scotland, so he brings a proper burr to the lead role, as well as doubling in several others—including a rare supplanting of Mickey's

regular portrayer, Jimmy McDonald. Donald Duck (Nephew) is played by his veteran voicer Clarence Nash, and Janet Waldo and Walker Edmiston perform admirably as well.

Goofy, Minnie, Merlin, and the Snow White Witch are on board, too; all in all, this is a tasty Yuletide pie of minced Disney & Dickens.

And with that one, we leave Kiddieland and return to Adult Town.

The *Carol*ers were busy there as well during this era, including in several solo performances—a return to the style of the earliest days of the tale's recording. That format choice may well have demonstrated the lingering echo of Dickens' own readings of the piece; because for years, the *Carol* seems to have been presented this way much more frequently than other comparable literary classics.

For instance, during this period we see no such proliferation of, say, Stoker's *Dracula* or Melville's *Moby Dick* in solo presentations.

One of the first of these "new old-style" recordings came from one of the most respected creators in the field, Arthur Luce Klein, by way of Spoken Arts and Argo records. "R.W." reviewed it in *Gramophone* magazine in 1959:

> "Surprisingly this is the first Christmas Carol on LP, although Bransby Williams is billed as Scrooge in a Dickens miscellany. Frank Pettingell has been a stalwart of the English stage for the best part of half a century, and ever a Dickensian. This is indeed a rather maudlin tale, but it is saved from going over the edge by the author's genius for local colour and by certain opportunities which any competent narrator (Dickens included) could seize. Mr. Pettingell will not disappoint either his or the story's admirers, and it only remains to say that the cuts are well arranged and the tale moves forward naturally to its touching close."

The Williams miscellany mentioned was a reissue package of his earlier shorts. And R.W. appears to disallow the previous Colman, Wyatt, Rathbone, and Barrymore record versions; perhaps because they originated not on LP but on 78 rpms, or because as audio plays he considered them "less pure" than readings. Or it may be that he was simply unaware of their existence. (No one writer possesses all the facts—please keep that in mind in the present case, dear reader.)

As we saw in the liner notes for his excellent 1941 production, Ernest Chappell had bemoaned the "confines of (this album's) forty minutes," and wished wistfully "that we could tell the tale in full, unhindered by the necessary mechanics which confound all methods of tale-telling."

In 1959, that wish finally came true for those who preferred their Dickens neat, not cut.

Over a century after the *Carol*'s publication, the *first* audio recording of its unabridged text.

Using the slow 16 2/3 rpm speed that fit twice as much material on a disc than the new LP standard of 33 1/3 rpm, the Audio Book Company presented the first recording of the unabridged text of Charles Dickens' *A Christmas Carol*, which clocks in at an impressive one hundred and eighty-four minutes.

Irish actor Dan O'Herlihy brings a strong voice to the telling, with just a pleasant hint of an accent. And he hits the "sweet spot" in two essential ways: his pace is just right, neither too fast nor too slow; and his performance strikes just the right balance between reading and acting. There is a good use of inflection in the differentiation of characters, with a gruff Scrooge, melancholy Marley, wistful Past

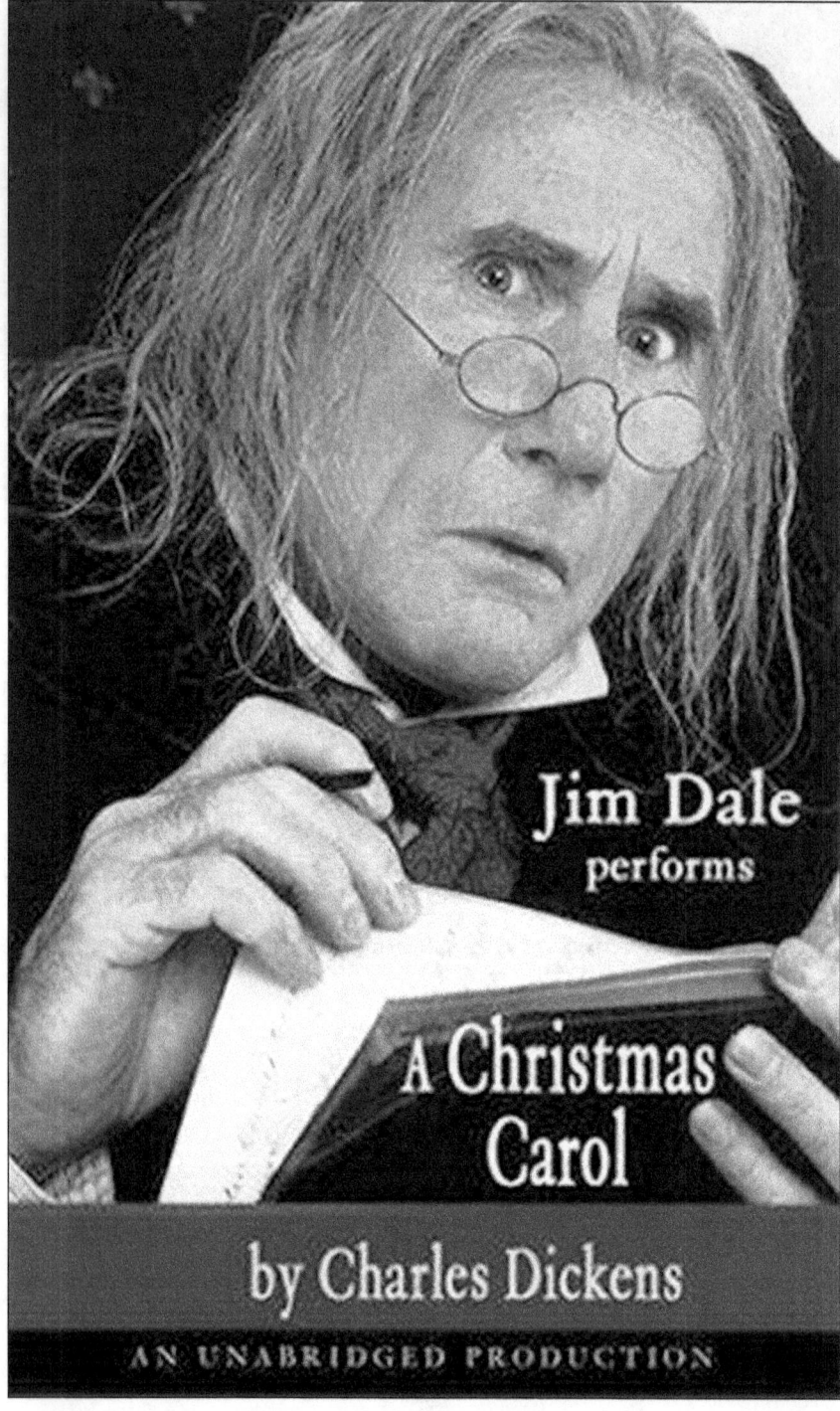

and fulsome Present. The actor does one of the finest jobs at the task at hand that this author has ever heard, making the production one of those rare instances in the arts where the first of a thing is also one of the very best. (Just two small glitches are to be found, for those who enjoy such trivia: an occasional page turn can be heard, and O'Herlihy delivers Dickens' early descriptive line about Scrooge, "He carried his own low temperature always about with him; he iced his office in the dogdays," as, "he iced his *coffee* in the dogdays." Perhaps more picturesque, but not from Dickens!)

This "Talking Book" was a real harbinger of the recorded book phenomenon that would come to take over the shelves of chain bookstores in the cassette and CD era, when it would be joined by unabridged *Carol*s from actors including Patrick Horgan, Geoffrey Palmer (of TV's *As Time Goes By*), Miriam Margolyes, and Jim Dale (of the stage's *Barnum*, and the *Harry Potter* films).

(A note that pertains here, as well as in the later Log section of the book: individual performances of the *Carol* can be almost as varied in style as are the people who do them. This ranges from a simple, literal reading of the text, to the full-out acting of the piece, with vocal differentiation for each character, changes of emotion, etc. The present author has tried where possible, to denote which is which, with such labels as "Reader" or "Solo Performance.")

There have also been many audio-recorded solo presentations using an edited rather than unabridged text, including several of Dickens' own public reading cut. Among these are performances by actors including Mark Redfield and Roy Dotrice.

Dotrice, known for his one-man Broadway *Mister Lincoln*, and as the Beast's father in the TV series *Beauty and the Beast*, actually added another layer to his performance by doing his reading in character as the original author. He also played Scrooge in a 1980 BBC radio version with songs, for which he utilizes an almost comically thin, reedy voice, probably to differentiate it from his "Dickens voice," which he uses when introducing the radio play with the introduction from the book.

Other readings/solo performances from streamlined texts include those done by non-actors, like that from the University of Florida's Dr. Lestor L. Hale in 1974. As in this case, such recordings often captured for posterity *Carol* presentations that had been done before

Roy Dotrice as Charles Dickens.

live audiences for years. Dean Hale had been reading the *Carol* publicly since at least 1932, and a non-commercial recording exists of his 1957 performance of the piece.

Then there are those that fall somewhere between reading and acting, by professional "storytellers" like Jim Weiss; and many more by seasoned actors such as Peter Bartlett, Anton Lesser, Tom Conti, and John Gielgud—the last, particularly well regarded.

And in addition to these and other solo editions, even as the classic radio era waned the record companies continued to produce "radio drama style" *Carols*, too.

In 1959 Top Rank/Vanguard brought forth one featuring Siobhan McKenna and a cast of Dublin actors including Milo O'Shea, with Anew McMaster as Scrooge. In an interesting choice, McKenna is cast as the "three-fold ghost"—but (thankfully!) after first calling Scrooge's name, Future remains mum.

In a syndicated AP review, Hugh Mulligan wrote that:

> "Dominick Roche's script pretends to stick faithfully to the original, but liberties have been taken throughout the whole production, the ending has been hooked [*sic*] up painfully and the sins of commission far exceed those of omission."

The present author would have to agree. There are bad shuffles and changes of the Dickens text throughout; i.e., Scrooge asking Cratchit to come in and work for a couple of hours on Christmas Day (!?) The recording does contain an "easter egg"-type hidden present for listeners who are fantasy/adventure fans, though—the production uses some of the same music library cues as the 1950s *Adventures of Superman* TV series.

And in 1960, the prestigious spoken word/ recorded drama label Caedmon produced a *Carol* with a storied British cast including Ralph Richardson as Scrooge, Frederick Treves, Norman Mitchell, Douglas Wilmer (BBC-TV's 1960s Sherlock Holmes) as Marley, and as "the Author and Narrator," Paul Scofield.

> "Now here comes Sir Ralph Richardson illuminating a narrative beautifully read by Paul Scofield. Sir Ralph is very fine here, particularly at the end, where his asides spell out the consummate actor that he is. This record is, of course, only of extracts, but the kernel of the story is here, and there is enough detail to give the flavour of the

writing.... My only complaint is that Marley's ghost is ludicrously overdrawn, but doubtless that is intended to frighten our listening children. On the other hand, the use of a solo violin neatly underlines the terror of old Ebenezer's solitary life—a good point this. Anybody still wanting a 'Christmas Carol' on disc will not be disappointed in this one."
—R.W., *Gramophone* magazine.

As mentioned before, Ralph Richardson was among that storied group of Twentieth Century British actors who were legendary for their long careers on stage, on the radio, and on television. And like Alec Guinness of that number, he was known for character work, rather than straight leads. With roles that ranged from the bizarre tyrant of H.G. Wells' *Things to Come* to Lord Fortnum of Alamein, who mutates into the title character of *The Bed Sitting Room*, Richardson was perhaps the quirkiest actor of the group, which fit him well for the portrayal of several Dickens figures including our beloved miser.

Sir Ralph had been acclaimed for his turn as Scrooge in U.S. Steel's first television presentation in 1952, for which he made a special trip to American shores, and where he was ably supported by a cast including such Hollywood Raj stalwarts as Arthur Treacher and Alan Napier. Though true to Caedmon's norm the 1960 records production is a bit "Masterpiece Theater austere" for this writer, the two giants of the stage onboard serve Mr. Dickens very well. Richardson would play Scrooge yet again, as well as narrate, in a solid BBC Radio offering for the 1965 holiday season; and narrator Paul Scofield, too, would record the piece again years later when he joined the ranks of solo *Carol*ers.

(And in yet another example of Dickensian symbiosis, *Carol*ers Harry Alan Towers, Orson Welles, and John Gielgud had worked with Richardson on a similarly iconic British property in their 1954 *Sherlock Holmes* radio series.)

Across the Atlantic in America during the same era that the Caedmon discs were produced, voice actors Peter Fernandez and Corinne Orr (both of *Speed Racer* and much, much more voice work) appeared in a Promotional LP version for the Franklin National Bank. It was produced by Herb Gale (Galewitz), who did several audio drama records in the 1960s that were very much in the radio style and used veteran radio actors. The featured characters were often those that had flourished on radio, such as Superman, Flash Gordon, and The Shadow (that one starring fellow record *Carol*er Brett Morrison.) The narrator here was Ray Heatherton, from a script based on Dickens' reading cut.

And up north in Canada, radio personality Carl Banas appeared on Polydor's *Charles Dickens' "A Christmas Carol" and other Yuletide Favorites*. As with several other *Carol*ers, Banas had previously performed live multi-voice readings of the story. American TV viewers may know him from another famous Christmas tale, the animated *Rudolph the Red-Nosed Reindeer*, where he plays the grumpy Head Elf; and he was also very good as Peter Parker's Scrooge-like boss J. Jonah Jameson in the first *Spider-Man* TV cartoon series.

And we close out our chapter on recorded *Carol*s by returning to a well-known one of the Solo variety:

Patrick Stewart is of course best known as *Star Trek: The Next Generation*'s Captain Jean-Luc Picard in the TV and motion picture series, as well as for other work in those media such as *I, Claudius* and *X-Men*. He is also a classically trained stage actor with decades of experience including several Shakespeare plays in England and New York, most recently *Macbeth*. And it was on stage that his *Carol* was born.

He adapted the text himself at a time when a one-man show with a limited schedule was perfect for an actor contracted to a seasonal TV series; and it is also a simple to stage voice-only production (there is a draft-of-cold-wind sound effect used to introduce the recorded version.)

The actor performed the piece from California to New York to London periodically from 1988 through 2005, and it was likely the publicity surrounding this production that inspired Turner Network Television's fully-produced TV movie *Carol* with Stewart in the lead in 1999.

This audio dramatization is very much of the Solo Performance rather than Reading variety. Stewart provides individualized voices for all his characters, right down to Tiny Tim. And his Broadway

work on this "one-hander" earned him a Drama Desk Award the same year that Simon & Schuster Audio produced the recording. Since its debut in 1991, it may well have supplanted the 1939 Barrymore/Welles version as the most popular audio *Carol*.

Of which we have seen that there are, like Christmas Present's elder brothers, a very great many!

But interestingly, though among that number there have been many uncut-text audio *Carol*s and many multi-cast audio *Carol*s, the present author could find no documentation for the production of an uncut AND multi-cast *Carol* before the modern mp3 era. But now that technology has made access to such long recordings easy and inexpensive, two such that can be found online include the one at Wired for Books directed by Karen M. Chan, and that at LibriVox produced by Elizabeth Klett.

In the liner notes for his 1947 recorded *Carol*, Lionel Barrymore said:

> "Charles Dickens' wonderful story has all the humour and whimsy and spirit of the season. It plays from your heartstrings to your backbone—and back again. We have tried to achieve the same effect in this album, and I think we have succeeded. The cast and the orchestra…have done a superb job in bringing (the)…warm and sensitive adaptation to life….
>
> I know you'll enjoy this album of Charles Dickens' 'A Christmas Carol'…enjoy it more and more…each time you play it."

That seems indeed to have been the happy outcome—and judging by their continuing production and reception, from many more recorded *Carol*s than just that disc set alone!

STAVE 6:
Christmas Present

"This particular Christmas Carol...combined the number one radio talk show host of the late Forties into the Sixties, with the leading talk host of the Seventies into the Nineties."

—William Nadel

And now, we turn back from commercial recordings to those *Carols* that soar through the air as freely as our favorite story's Spirits do.

Moving through the 1950s into the 1960s, we enter the period when broadcast drama was being shifted by the networks to television in favor of radio—but the Spirits of Christmas seem to have gained a special stay of execution for audio broadcasts of our tale. As Bill points out above, even when considering recent times we are still able to shift our focus back from records "to *radio* Carols, which did *not* die...!"

The birthplace of Lionel Barrymore's Scrooge, the Columbia Broadcasting System, even gave his 1947 MGM records edition a network showcase several years after the actor's death. Hosted by no less an eminence than Sir Cedric Hardwicke, this was the 1957 broadcast alluded to by producer Dailey Paskman in his comments in the previous chapter. And NBC honored that same production by featuring a slightly edited version of it on their last-gasp network radio omnibus *Monitor*, hosted by TV gameshow host Gene Rayburn on Christmas Day of 1965.

Continuing on through the decade between 1955 and 1965, many stations aired that very same Barrymore *Carol* locally. In fact in Orange, Virginia, WJMA station owner Arch Harrison handpicked it from among several to air in 1961, and repeated it every Christmas Eve during his tenure until 1984.

Others preferred one of Ronald Colman's two productions, as in the case of WVNJ, Newark, New Jersey. More than once, they presented his 1941 version as the centerpiece of a novel program, bracketing it with carols from around the world performed by the Rutgers University Glee Club.

Back in the land of the story's birth, where the BBC had not decimated their radio networks to fund their new television ones, radio drama continued in much greater force than in the States. And Yuletide 1965 in Merrie Present England saw the return of star Ralph Richardson to the role he'd played earlier for Caedmon records.

Interestingly, though Richardson narrates this time as well in his own straight voice, he actually uses less elderly stridence for his Scrooge than in the earlier portrayal. Returning with him from that production is Fredrick Treves, promoted here from Fred to Bob, and the actor does as fine a job in the new role as he had in the previous one, creating another well-defined character. The rest of the seasoned British cast is good as well; though in what may have been a directorial choice, the Ghosts—John Ruddock's Marley, Wilfrid Carter's Past, and Ralph Truman's Present—are all ephemeral almost to the point of feeble (thank goodness, Future does not speak.)

But it's a worthy production overall, utilizing a solid adaptation (by Charles Lefeaux?) that retains much of the original.

"The Beeb" in the modern era also brought us excerpts from the *Carol* on *Story Time* featuring Patrick Magee, as well as the musicalized Roy Dotrice Scrooge mentioned in the previous chapter. And in 1990, fantasy genres cross-pollinated yet again, as a veteran of England's Hammer Studios' horror films who also played Bruce Wayne's butler presented us with his take on literature's most famous covetous old sinner.

Of course British Malaya-born Michael Gough (sadly, another *Carol*er who died even as this project was taking shape) did a great deal more than that in a sixty-two-year career that ranged not only from *Horror of Dracula* to *Batman*, but also from fellow-Scrooge Laurence Olivier's *Richard III* to Chekov's *The Cherry Orchard*.

His *Carol* is narrated by his fellow Hammer films veteran Freddie Jones, and sports another great Anglo cast including Vivian Pickles and Timothy Bateson (from Dotrice's musicalization.) And Nephew Fred here is Douglas Hodge, who in another example of the synergy within the world of audio *Carol*s (this time, connected to the 1959

O'Herlihy recording), is active in the Royal National Institute of Blind People's "Talking Books" program due to the vision disability of his grandmother.

Another nicely scripted *Carol*, this one also has the rare benefit of a full hour and a half running time. And it is very much what is commonly called a "Modern Audio Drama": the ambient sound quality and the somewhat underplayed acting style, all presented in crisp stereo, give the production a film-like "realism" (though in drama that is a subjective term of course, debatable at another time.) Such qualities likely make this one a very accessible version for contemporary listeners, especially the young. In some ways, it is analogous to George C. Scott's admirable TV movie edition from the around the same time and place (and Gough appeared in that one, as well.)

As a radio announcer might say "moving on to National news of the day...."

Though the year 1962 is generally considered the marker for the sharpest decline in the amount of dramatic radio in America, the flotilla of *Carol*s in the crisp Yuletide ether have continued to sail on with gusto since that time. In fact amazingly, the modern era has actually seen the premiere of new NETWORK productions of the holiday classic.

Veteran producer Himan Brown's (*Inner Sanctum*, etc.) *CBS Radio Mystery Theater* was one of the last attempts by the American commercial networks to maintain/revive radio drama. As such, it is beloved of many TV-era children as their first tempting taste of that delicious medium. Only once during the long run of the series did host E.G. Marshall play a character role in addition to narrating, and it was for this special Christmas episode in 1975—a *Carol* which would be repeated every December of the series' run its last in 1982.

Marshall makes a fine—and fun—Scrooge. He's supported by Tony Award winner Marian Seldes, and classic radio era veterans Evie Juster, William Redfield, Robert Dryden, and Ian Martin, who also wrote the quite serviceable script. Ye author's only quibble: the adaptation and production are a bit—"stingy?"—and that characteristic of Scrooge's should not carry over to presentations of his story. There's not one young person in the cast. It's bad enough to not have a Turkey Boy at the end of the tale; but the voices supposed to be those of the Cratchit children are only heard indistinctly—including that of Tiny Tim himself!

Come 1990, National Public Radio mounted a unique production with Jonathan Winters and Mimi Kennedy. It is based upon Dickens' reading version, and Winters plays the story straight, though his patented quirkiness of character is very much in place. As of the writing of this book, the show is still a Public Radio perennial.

And several not-quite-network but very-widely-syndicated *Carols* have been produced in U.S. in the modern era as well. Christmas 1983 saw one on stations who carry programming from the NPR-related organization American Public Radio.

In addition, the several hundred stations that carry *Focus on the Family Radio Theatre* have aired a production that originated in 1996, and that like NPR's is still being heard to the present day.

As with all of that series' offerings, their version of Dickens' classic is very well produced, much in the Modern Audio Drama style described above concerning the Gough production. The host is well-known TV Hercule Poirot, David Suchet, and among the all-British cast of this London production is narrator Timothy Bateson, who as well as *Carol*ing in that Gough edition, was in Dotrice's before that—yes, the Radio *Carol* Stock Company tradition continues. And in still more *Carol* interconnectedness, the script by Paul McCusker uses as source material not only Dickens' book, but also Noel Langley's acclaimed screenplay for the classic 1951 Alistair Sim film *Scrooge* (known in the U.S., of course, as *A Christmas Carol*.)

In addition, as of this writing in the Year of our Lord 2012, national radio programming source the Public Radio Exchange carries three separate productions of the timeless tale (more about one of those in the next chapter).

And then there is the occasional strange hybrid *Carol*...

One such was composed of the songs from Basil Rathbone's 1956 TV musical *The Stingiest Man in Town*, with linking narration spoken by John Carradine (who had earlier himself played Scrooge in a 1947 live TV broadcast.)

There exists a commercial recording of this, as well an anecdotal account from radio historian William Nadel about a broadcast on

Basil Rathbone, radio and record Scrooge, in character for the first of his two television performances of the role. Martyn Green is poor Bob Cratchit. (1956)

Florida radio around Christmas of 1971. It may well have been in conjunction with a performance of this *Stingiest* script that Carradine did on stage in New York that season, narrated by Mayor John Lindsay.

And Bob Statzer, chronicler of cinematic Scrooges, tells us of another "combination *Carol*":

> "Back in the Seventies, right after the 1970 Albert Finney musical version of *Scrooge* had its network television debut, I remember a radio broadcast of Lionel Barrymore's version of *A Christmas Carol* into which had been incorporated some of the musical numbers from the Finney film."

(The Finney film's first telecast was by NBC on December 23, 1974.)

In addition to these trend-bucking network broadcasts and unique mutant productions, the tradition of home-grown local radio *Carols* has continued in an unbroken line down from WEAF's in 1922. These local shows are legion, so we will touch on just a few here, and interested persons can turn to the Log for many more.

In 1965, KPFK Los Angeles aired a *Carol* created by Henry Miller and one David Ossman, soon to be famous as a founding member of the Firesign Theatre. The station's "Radio Repertory" cast featured Norman Belkin, who later wrote for such TV programs as *All in the Family*.

Too, many have been performed by local on-air station staffs around the country. Sometimes, these have added yet another timeless truth to the many that the *Carol* furnishes: that announcing, disc jockeying, and acting are not exactly the same gifts, and are not always found in the same person! Some Locals include:

1965: WTOD-AM & FM, Toledo, Ohio, with The WTOD Players...

1978: WMMG, Brandenburg, Kentucky and the Kentucky Network, Inc., live from Diners Playhouse, Lexington...

1979: KGO, San Francisco, featuring "Mayor" Art Finley, Al "Jazzbeaux" Collins, and Jay Schneider. The program is introduced as live without rehearsal, and that fact is amply demonstrated by the looseness of the performance and the

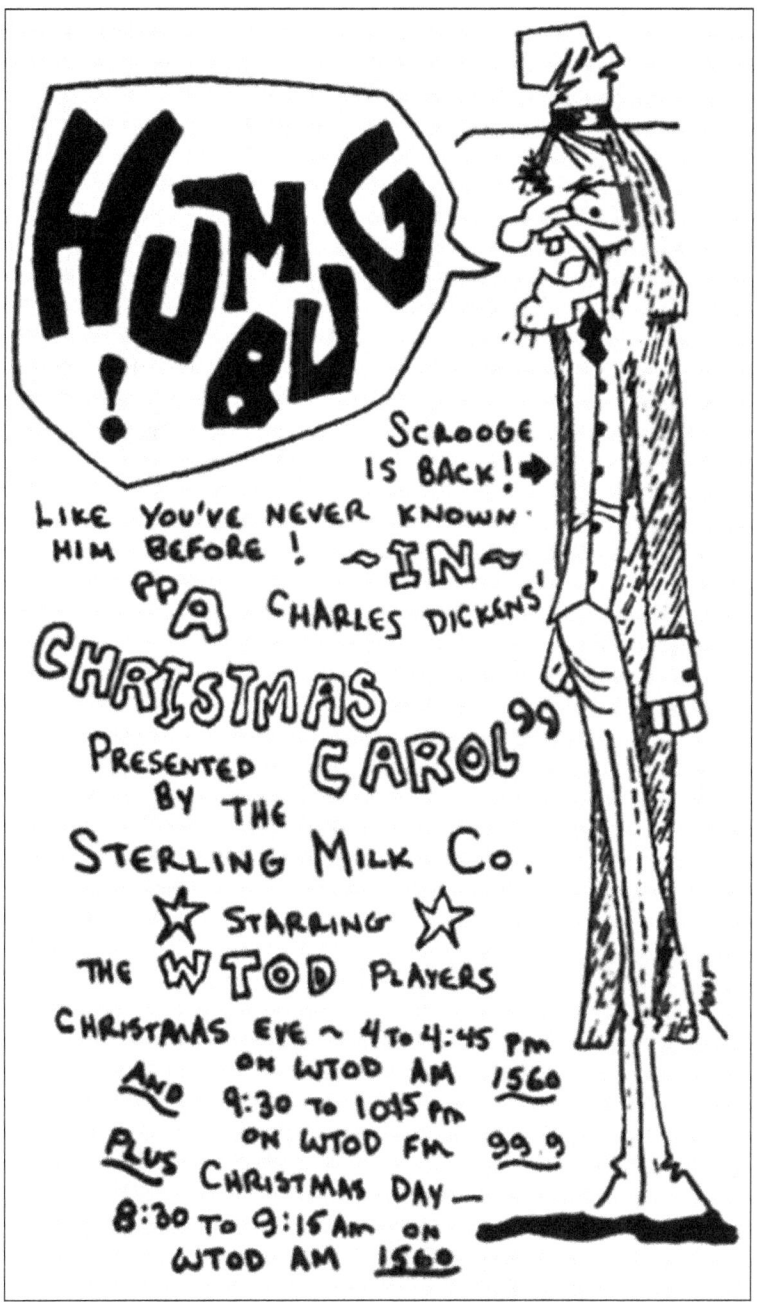

many on-mike breakups. But even this "festive" *Carol* was trumped by a similar one from the Windy City nine years later.

"God Save Us, Every One! Dahl Makes Mincemeat Of A Classic" toplined the article by Steve Johnson in the Chicago Tribune that December 23rd, and it seems that the merrie revelers of WLUP-AM that season tried to out-party even the folks at Fezziwig's, perhaps with help from a few bowls of... steaming Christmas punch?

Before a small live audience at the Museum of Broadcast Communications, radio personality Steve Dahl,

> "...established himself as perhaps the finest actor ever to play Scrooge in a Hawaiian shirt...(in a presentation of Dickens' tale)... interpreted with a generosity befitting the season, and a fatuosity befitting a bad critic.
>
> The script, provided by the Goodman Theatre (currently doing its annual, less adventuresome version of the play), received a treatment not unlike that of a fish in the maw of a walrus...the whole production had an unrehearsed quality that would have been quite impressive had it not, in fact, been unrehearsed.... The cast read blatantly and haphazardly from the 'scripts,' tearing pages off and tossing them aside as they 'finished,' speaking from time to time in flaming non sequiturs as they pretended (very realistically) to lose their place....
>
> Holding the many disparate elements together was the mind of Dahl, who played Scrooge as an irreverent radio host playing Scrooge.... A good portion of (his) performance, though, was spent trying to illuminate the heretofore undiscovered sexual subtext of Dickens' work...(along with) frequent references to bodily functions...."

We can't be sure what Mr. Dickens would have thought of this public beating (—er—) "reading" of his little Carol. But it sounds as if it was a joyous occasion for those present, both in front of the mike and behind it, where many Chicago media personalities, including movie critic Rogert Ebert, as the Ghost of Christmas Past, found themselves.

Most other local *Carol*s have trod the straight and narrow, though.

One such was produced at the very station mentioned at the beginning of this tome that blessed this listener with his introduction to Lionel Barrymore's Classic '39 in the early 1970s. Come Christmas of 1981, it offered its own new home-grown edition of Dickens' story.

WOWO Ft. Wayne (Indiana) air all-stars including Ron Gregory, Jack Underwood, Bob Sievers, and "Young Chris" Roberts performed the story this time out. Sievers was a local legend who had been at the station since 1932, and who had already earned his Yuletide bona fides by starting the annual "Penny Pitch" holiday charity drive with fellow long-timer Jay Gould. And Roberts, though perhaps not quite as "Young" now, is still in radio in the area as of this writing. The original script for the production was written by Walter Hackett, and the show was produced by Tim Goeglein and Jim Skimos, still students at the time.

Another among the other such local *Carol*s, WBZ Boston's 1999 version with Gary LaPierre leading "The WBZ Holiday Players" as Scrooge, has aired several times since its debut. And as that one moves us to the bigger East Coast markets, special mention is due two unique *Carol*s from that region that featured names known well beyond their local stations' coverage.

WNBC New York, the flagship station of the network, presented a new production of the ghost story on Christmas Eve of 1970 with a variegated cast that featured Marv Albert, the sportscaster later known for a scandal involving the more intimate sports; Charles McCord, soon to begin a long stint as sidekick to Don Imus; and Long John Nebel (born John Zimmerman) the subtitle of whose biography describes him as "radio talk king, master salesman, and magnificent charlatan."

Nebel was a groundbreaker for the late-night broadcast mavens to come after him, with programming ranging from books to horse racing, and from UFOs (which subject he discussed with no less a polymath than Jackie Gleason!) to conspiracy theories. In fact, Nebel's own wife Candy Jones claimed to have undergone CIA mind control experiments. And in the ongoing string of *Carol* synergies, it is Jones who links us with the next one we'll cover.

Over to you, radio historian William Nadel, for more about the *Carol* you mentioned at the beginning of this chapter:

> "I think I listened to this one, with Bob Grant, on WMCA in December of 1980 or '81. It didn't make a big impression at the time (I mean, you know, I've heard so many of these things!) But here's the significance of it....
>
> You see, Barry Gray had initiated the modern talk radio school of interviewing people and taking calls from listeners, in New York on WOR and then WMCA. And his career was cut short by a fall in a Chinese restaurant that more or less put him out of commission for a while. So Bob Grant, who had started in the late Sixties/early Seventies in California as I guess you would call him the 'fill-in host' for Joe Pyne, came to New York from the West Coast in about '75–'76—and *he* became the leading talk host.
>
> Candy Jones was in this *Christmas Carol* too, who was the wife of Long John Nebel. (The Nebel show was on WMCA, the two of them did the show together, and when he died, it became The Candy Jones Show.) Many of these people went basically from WOR to WMCA to ABC as the formats changed to talk; and also featured in this show was Mark Simone, who took over from Bob Grant through the late Eighties and Nineties.

So this one combined the talk radio hosts of yesterday, with those still on the air today!"

The production Bill speaks of does indeed feature Gray, Grant, Jones, and Simone, all in one big "Talk Radio *Carol*." The script used is not the strongest; and in this author's opinion, the production proves once again that acting and announcing/speaking on mike are separate disciplines, and that few people are gifted in both (with the occasional rare exception like Jackson Beck, Ernest Chappell, and Bill Owen).

But Grant actually had some experience in the acting field when he was young, and his performance in the lead is solid. The same cannot be said for many of his fellow castmates, a few of whom evidently fell into the most deadly trap there is for a prospective audio performer—thinking, "it is just *reading*, right?"

Now, if the previous show was a "Talk Radio *Carol*," then the next was a "Rock Radio *Carol*."

In 1980, New York's progressive rock station WNEW-FM presented Scott Muni as Scrooge in a cast that included fellow "free-form" disk jockeys Vin Scelsa, Dennis Elsas, and Pete Fornatale (another *Carol*er who passed to the next world during the creation of this study). Though not credited as such (probably intentionally) the script used is the trustworthy one from the 1941/1949 Colman production; and though the acting might not be what one would get from such as Barrymore, Chappell, Moorehead, and Kearns, it is a cut above that in most of the station staff productions listed above. All involved seem to take Mr. Dickens and the season seriously.

And, as ever, when a group does that, it shows.

And on that note dear reader, as we move through Christmas Past's purview into Christmas Present's, if you will indulge an old *Carol*er for just a few moments longer I would like to detail the genesis of just one more producer's efforts....

STAVE 7:
May that be truly said of us

"The evil Scrooge, much like Dickensian England itself, needed a strong shock to the system to see the light.... Quicksilver's production brings back the necessary 'fear factor' in order for the audience to appreciate not only what Dickens was trying to accomplish, but HOW."
—*Richard Pirodsky, KKFI.*

(Thank you, Richard. We have spent a good deal of this study discussing the external details of various iterations of Dickens' masterwork, and as we approach the finish, it is good to be reminded again of its heart and soul.)

Your present author has loved the *Carol* as long as he can recall, beginning when he was four years old and watched the premiere of very first animated-for-television holiday special, *Mr. Magoo's Christmas Carol*. To my mind, it is still one of the very best filmed versions, and THE best musical version. And when I first encountered Mr. Dickens' perfect jewel of a book itself, by way of Ronald Searle's illustrated version in our school's library, I was as thrilled as countless others have been since that fabled Christmas of 1843.

Not long after that, I was Scrooge in a fellow student's unfinished 8mm *Carol* epic in High School. And after a stint at NYU and the Stella Adler School of Acting, I first had the chance to play the role fully in 1994 when I produced a live-on-stage recreation of Welles' 1939 show, ably directed by my friend William Rogers as a benefit for Christ Lutheran Church in Manhattan.

And the next year, I had the high honor to join the company of some of the illustrious folks we've covered earlier in this book, by producing my own broadcast radio version. This was by way of WBAI-FM in New York, which had proudly continued to hold the torch of radio drama in general, and of *Carol*s in specific, aloft after the networks had largely abandoned them; and also by the good graces of one of WBAI's most stalwart veterans in that crusade, Max Schmid.

That first production of our Quicksilver Radio Theater group was directed by my friend Jay Stern (of the upcoming film *The Adventures of Paul and Marian*), and he recalls:

> "When Craig Wichman asked me to direct a radio production of *A Christmas Carol*, I had two major reservations: first, I had a film degree and had recently begun directing theater, but radio drama was entirely outside of my experience—not just as a director, but also as an audience member; second, as a Jew, I had little interest and even a bit of aversion to the plays, movies, and TV specials awash with the 'message of Christmas' that seem to flood the airwaves for a good ninety days of the year. So between the format (how to tell a story with just sound) and the context (something about the example of the baby Jesus bringing salvation to sinners?), I felt I was entirely unsuited to the project.
>
> But Craig persisted. He and I had worked together on a few stage projects, and he felt I had the skill to pull it off. My skepticism about the material was also a benefit considering Craig's approach—he wanted to strip away the sentimentalism and non-Dickensian aspects that *A Christmas Carol* has taken on over the years, and to go back to the story that the author wrote."

(Hopefully somewhere out there Harold Loekle and Ernest Chappell, who spoke so eloquently in earlier pages about the importance of properly honoring sterling source material like the *Carol*, smile down…)

> "Once I actually read Dickens' tale I was convinced to do it. It's a great story, and

wonderfully structured; it's dark, very sad, and the tears of joy at the end are hard-earned and genuine. Plus there's a lot of room to create spooky atmosphere and ghost effects!

Craig's adaptation of the story went a long way in helping to imagine the audio world of the piece. His script indicated what we would rely on narration and dialogue to convey, while opening up possibilities for certain moments to be expressed entirely through sound. It turned out that my film background was a benefit: sound design is a major part of film production, and a big trick of low budget projects is to use sound to make the movie feel bigger—if you only have a few extras for a crowd scene, you can use sound to expand it. Can't afford a restaurant location? Stick a table in the corner of your apartment and add restaurant ambience on the soundtrack.

Also, with audio drama, my technical side was able to achieve the kind of perfection in timing and control that I couldn't on the stage. In Dickens' story, characters and locations transform instantly, and a well-placed gust of wind can achieve that with great economy and maximum effect. Creating the effect of Scrooge shoving the Ghost of Christmas Past down into its cone-shaped hat would be a monster to stage or film, but in audio drama, a music cue and vocalizations from the actors make it happen magically in the mind of the audience.

And it's easy to chill people with the use of just a human voice.... Dickens' narrator tells the reader that he is 'standing in the spirit at your elbow,' and when you hear that whispered to you when you have headphones on, it can be a very creepy moment indeed.

One of the big challenges for a director and cast several of whom have no previous experience working in, or even listening to, audio drama is how to convert an acting performance to the medium. How do you show a glance with a grunt? How can characters make their presence felt in a scene when they're not speaking? And how do you 'block' for radio, when the only space is the air between the actor and the microphone? We felt this out bit by bit, as we started rehearsing; sometimes the vocal hems and haws may be a bit too much in our first few shows, but gradually over several we found the right balance.

And with *A Christmas Carol* and our other Quicksilver shows, we've developed a method which is not common among other audio drama groups—we have a rehearsal where we actually block the scenes out. Actors get a chance to physically move around, sit and stand accordingly, and set the physical distance between them and their fellow actors within the scene. Then when we get to the microphone, the actors know if they need to whisper or shout to be heard, and they know their proper distance to each other, as expressed in their distance from the mike.

Two things opened up to me with this project: the rich world of Dickens' story, and the even richer medium of audio drama, which has served me well in both stage and film.

Craig Wichman (Scrooge) and John Prave (Bob Cratchit) on mike, and director Jay Stern in the control room, at the legendary old WBAI studios in New York. (Here working on Quicksilver Radio Theater's *Frankenstein*, the Halloween after Quicksilver's Christmas debut with the *Carol*.)

Audio drama asks directors to be very imaginative and to embrace simplicity, and that economy has helped inform my other work. One big lesson I learned from directing this play is to never judge source material by its adaptations. Go straight to the original. If a piece is constantly re-adapted, there has to be something in the original that exceeds them all and is worth revisiting, no matter your background or expectations."

Thanks again, partner, for a job very well done.

I am fiercely proud of the sterling work done by our cast: Anthony Cinelli, John Prave, Ghislaine Nichols, Deborah Barta, Joseph Franchini, Jodi Botelho, Elizabeth Stull, and Tony Scheinman. Their work was topped off and unified by the original music score from Tony Award-winner Mark Hollmann, and the rich sound effects by Clyde Baldo and the cast, all blended into one whole by the sound engineering talents of the late David Nolan.

Speaking for myself, this actor considers it a sort of sacred honor to play roles like Ebenezer Scrooge. And as Jay said, in my adaptation we tried to remove the quaint "Disneyfication" often added to the piece, and to return to it the grit and fear of what its author had, after all, considered a "ghost story." And thankfully, we were among the lucky *Carol*ers who have had a full hour to tell Dickens' well-textured tale.

We've been very heartened by the wonderful response "our little *Carol*" has gotten down through the seventeen years since its birth.

> "This charming adaptation of 'A Christmas Carol' would warm even Scrooge's heart, another in a line of Quicksilver's quality radio adaptations."
> —Michael Rogers, *Library Journal*.

> "Highly produced, full-out radio—to die for!"
> —Matthew Finch, WBAI-FM.

Stafford Township Historical Society
Dickens: A Christmas Carol
and Sing-a-long
Friday December 12, 2003 at 7:00 PM
at the Old Baptist Church, Rt 9 Manahawkin
Sponsored by: THE VAN DYK GROUP
Simulcast on 90.7 WYRS
016 016
COST: $ 5.00

And most touching of all, several listeners have told us that our *Carol* has become a part of their annual holiday tradition.

The production has the honor of being made a part of the collection of the Paley Center for Media. And it can still be heard today by way of iTunes, and on-air by way of the Public Radio Exchange—yes, radio stations WILL still present audio drama, old and new, but they need YOUR encouragement to do so. And of course, copies can be acquired directly from its producer.

In 2003, Quicksilverites Dan Renkin, Eevin Hartsough, and Bernadette Fiorella accompanied me to Manahawkin, New Jersey, where we were joined by local players including Rick Mellerup, Nick Feeney, and Mayor Carl Block in presenting a new broadcast *Carol*. We were hosted by the Stafford Township Historical Society before an appreciative audience at the wonderful site of the historic Old Baptist Church—which was already eighty years old when Dickens sat down to write his tale! Our production aired live on Bob Wick's WYRS, and since airtime was not as tight as usual on the independent station carrying us, I was happy to be able to fit even more of the original author's words into the script than was the case with our 1995 production.

I do not expect to match Lionel Barrymore's run with the piece— but I hope it is given to me to be able to continue to celebrate the *Carol* for a long time to come. Holiday season 2010 saw the premiere of my short film *A Christmas Carol—In Eight Minutes*; produced with the aid of one Master Jay Stern, it compresses many of the best film versions into one breakneck, all-star, *Carol*ette.

Then of course, there's this humble tome. And as of this writing, Quicksilver is scheduled to celebrate our own seventeenth anniversary in tandem with Mr. Dickens' two-hundredth by way of a new live *Carol* this Advent in Episcopal Actors' Guild Hall, at New York City's historic Little Church Around The Corner.

In addition, the gracious hosts of *Radio Once More* have asked me for the last several years to do a webcast each Yuletide on the subject of radio/audio *Carols*. Of course, the World Wide Web is one of the most common venues for these Dickensian productions now—both archived versions of many of the classic shows we have covered here, as well as new ones born every holiday season, are there presented as live Webcasts, accessible Podcasts, and shared digital files to be downloaded.

Yes, as mentioned way back at the beginning of this study, radio, that new child of the early Twentieth Century, has lived long enough now to spawn its own "grandchildren" media. In recent years, new *Carols* in such venues have included the Sirius/XM *satellite* radio premiere in 2004 of the Colonial Radio Theatre's production, as well as Spoken Word America's webcast debut of one from 2007 by the Night Kitchen Radio Theater.

You may recall that several chapters ago we promised the Mercury Theatre's Ghost of Christmas Past 1938 a few more words. Arthur Anderson, you're on:

> "In 2010 Don Connelly from Western Carolina University contacted the Orson Welles archive in Bloomington, Indiana. He was able to get access to the original 1938 script with all the typos and misspellings and the original cast, and they found that I was one of the few Mercury Players who was still alive.
>
> And they called me from down there and said, 'Do you have a significant other you would like to bring?' I said, 'My wife of forty-seven years, yes.' So Alice and I both went and it was a marvelous adventure. And

```
COLUMBIA BROADCASTING SYSTEM
THE CAMPBELL PLAYHOUSE
FRIDAY, DECEMBER 23rd, 1938
9:00 to 10:00 P.M.
CUE:                (COLUMBIA BROADCASTING SYSTEM)
                    (...........30 seconds.......)
MUSIC:              FANFARE
                        ANNC'R
The makers of Campbell's Soups present -- THE CAMPBELL PLAYHOUSE!
......Orson Welles, producer.
MUSIC:      TCHAIKOWSKY THEME (OR CHRISTMAS CAROL) AND FADE FOR:
                        ANNC'R
Tonight Orson Welles and the Campbell Playhouse observe a Campbell
tradition of long standing.  They bring you Charles Dickens' well-
loved tale of yuletide, "A Christmas Carol".

Four years ago the makers of Campbell's Soups went shopping for
a Christmas present to give to all their friends.  They found it
in this story, Charles Dickens' embodiment of the very spirit of
Christmas.  And they chose well, because throughout the country
today - in thousands of homes - it has become and beloved
Christmas custom, to listen to this story.

Tonight, this fourth annual presentation is brought to you with the
sincere wish that your Christmas may be a happy one, and with the
hope that the re-telling of "A Christmas Carol", may help to
make it so.
```

Original mimeoed script from 1938 which answered the call of the *Carol* again in 2010. (Courtesy of the Lilly Library, Indiana University, Bloomington, Indiana; Campbell Soup Company, and Don Connelly of Western Carolina University.)

Original talented actor from 1938 who answered the call of the *Carol* again in 2010—Arthur Anderson. (Courtesy of Western Carolina University.)

it was done in a beautiful theater with full orchestra, cast, and sound effects. The actors were mostly from among the faculty and students, and they were in general excellent. Really in a way the experience was new... I was happy to be experiencing it again, but the Ghost of Christmas Past was a new part after all these years!"

(And Mr. Anderson is scheduled to don those glittering robes for yet a third time, Ghosting again as Quicksilver's special guest star come December of 2012.)

As work on this book was beginning in New York City in 2011, the Yuletide found Oscar winner F. Murray Abraham playing the squeezing, wrenching, grasping, scraping, clutching, covetous old sinner before a live audience for broadcast over WQXR/WNYC. And out across the waves on Long Island in the Hamptons, the venerable 1939 Mercury script received the breath of life again by way of a new WPPB production.

And so in closing, we round this story like an "O"…

As I drove to and from Candlelight Services back home in Northwest Ohio on the crisp, starlit Christmas Eve of 2011, several Scrooges and company flew in through the car radio….

The quirky Jonathan Winters production, from a local NPR station… All the way from New Orleans' WWL (on that clear Midwinter air which is so conducive to AM radio waves), the *Focus on the Family* edition… And last but best, Barrymore and Welles' 1939 triumph, from Chicago. Quicksilver's show was being carried that Christmas by WGBH, WRNC, and WAMU; and myriad other *Carol*s, both old and new, were hurtling through the skies like the Ghosts of Christmas, all across America.

The piercing morality tale that young Charles Dickens brought forth from the depths of his soul, that spans past, present and future to remind us of the eternal consequences of our everyday actions, still feeds *our* souls today.

Upon the beloved authors' death in 1870, a poor London child asked a stranger, "Dickens dead? Then will Father Christmas die too?"

NO.

The Father Christmas-like Spirit of Christmas Present, and his child *A Christmas Carol*, are still bursting with life nearly a century and a half later—as are the audio dramatizations of the tale, now a century old themselves.

And these things will live forever, in the hearts of everyone who knows how to keep Christmas well—if anyone alive possesses that knowledge.

And so, as Tiny Tim observed, "God bless us, every one!"

Appendix:
"MANY CALLS SCROOGE MADE THAT NIGHT..."

A (Yule) Log of Broadcast and For Home Use Audio Productions (chiefly American) of Charles Dickens' *A Christmas Carol.*

Unless noted, all productions listed are direct presentations of the story rather than variations on it, and multiple cast rather than single reader; and times given are Eastern Standard. Generally, credits are as found in the original sources; and comments by others are in quotations, with comments by the present author in parentheses. The majority of the pieces listed are Broadcasts; in order to differentiate Commercial Recordings, they are headlined in **BOLD** type. Where available, the location of a given station will follow its call letters when it first appears in this list.

GLOSSARY OF ABBREVIATIONS (Following each term's first use in this log, it will generally be abbreviated thereafter.)

Ancr. – ANNOUNCER
Dir. – DIRECTOR
Cond. – CONDUCTOR/CONDUCTED
Min. – MINUTES
Mus. – MUSIC
Narr. – NARRATOR
Prd. – PRODUCER
Sec. – SECONDS
Sfx. – SOUND EFFECTS
Spons. – SPONSOR
Synd. – SYNDICATED/SYNDICATION
Wr. – WRITER

Circa 1905 – The first audio-recorded portrayal of Ebenezer Scrooge:

1904–06? – **STERLING RECORDS**, #276. Cylinder. (2 min. 18 sec.) "Scrooge's Christmas Morning." (aka "Scrooge's Awakening," the title announced on the recording.) *Cast:* Scrooge, Albert Whelan; "Boy"; Chorus. (The Carter catalog [see Sources] documents a release date of Jan. 1906; but other sources differ as to date.)

1905 – British **EDISON RECORDS**, #13353. Cylinder. "Scrooge's Awakening." *Music. Cast:* Scrooge, Bransby Williams; "Boy"; Chorus.

(The dates given for the recordings above vary by sources; so until definitive confirmation, we will grant Mssrs. Williams and Whelan a tie for "First" in this case.)

1916 – **VICTOR RECORDS**, # 35566. "Scrooge (Part 1 – Marley's Ghost; Part 2 – The Ghost of Christmas Past)." *Solo Performance:* William Sterling Battis. *Mus.:* Violin, Ted Levy; Traps, William H. Reitz.

12-22-1922 – WEAF, New York. 7:15-7:45pm. *Reader:* Charles Mills. *Music:* Grace McDermott, violinist; Mary Burgum, pianist.
– "Today's Radio Program," New York Times 12-22-1922

12-24-1922 – KYW, Chicago. 11:30pm-12:30am. *Reader:* Gloria Chandler.
   "…Rev. Gardner A. MacWhorter, rector of St. Edmunds Episcopal church, will read the gospel story of Christ's nativity and the St. Edmunds choir will sing. Miss Gloria Chandler will also read Charles Dickens' 'Christmas Carol.'"
– "News Of The Religious World" column, Chicago Tribune
    12-17-1922

12-17-1923 – WOR, Newark, N.J. 8:10-8:35pm. *Lecturer?:* Tom Terris.
   "Tom Terris on Characters from Dickens' Christmas Carol"
– Bridgeport Telegram 12-27-1923

12-20-1923 – WLW, Cincinatti. 10pm. *Reader:* Prof. Van Wye, University of Cincinnati. (Part of Christmas program)
– (Cleveland) Plain Dealer 12-20-1923

12-23-1923 – CKY, Winnipeg. Pm. *Reader:* Rev. E. F. Church.
"...from Fort Rouge Methodist church on Sunday evening a special musical programme has been prepared by the choir... The pastor, Rev. E. F. Church, will, by special request, recite Dickens' 'Christmas Carol' in place of the usual sermon."
– Winnipeg Free Press 12-22-1923

12-24-1923 – WEAF. 11:20am-12pm. *Reading/Music.*
– "Today's Radio Program," New York Times 12-24-1923

12-24-1923 – WGY, Schenectady. 7:45pm. *Reader:* Edward H. Smith.
"Musical program...WGY orchestra... St. Ann's choir boys, Asa O. Coggeshall, director ... reading, 'Christmas Carol' (Dickens), Stave the First, Edward H. Smith...."
– (Cleveland) Plain Dealer 12-24-1923

12-24-1923 – WRC, Wash., D.C. 9:30-9:55pm. *Reading.*
– "Today's Radio Program," New York Times 12-24-1923

12-25-1923 – WLAG, Minneapolis. Pm. *Format?*
"Dickens' 'Christmas Carol,' incorporated in a surprise variety programme, is the piece de resistance for Christmas afternoon."
– Manitoba Free Press 12-22-1923

01-21-1924 – WMC, Memphis. 9pm. *Lecturer:* Frederick D. Losey.
"...on 'A Christmas Carol,' by Charles Dickens."
– Boston Globe 01-20-1924

12-19-1924 – WGY. 8:15pm. *Reader:* Edward H. Smith. *Mus.:* WGY Orchestra.
– Springfield (MA) Republican 12-14-24, Trenton Evening Times 12-19-1924

12-19-1924 – WOAW, Omaha. 10-10:30pm Central. *Solo Performance:* Ernest R. Misner, Misner School of Spoken Word. "Impersonations from (Dicken's 'Christmas Carol')"
– Boston Globe, Seattle Daily Times 12-19-1924

12-22-24 – WOR. 9:30-9:45pm. *Lecture?*
   "Dickens' Christmas Carols and Old London Types"
– Bridgeport Telegram, Lowell (MA) Sun 12-22-1924

12-24-1924 – WEAF. 7:30-8:15pm. *Reader:* Charles Howard Mills. *Mus.:* Frieda Lehman, violin; Ruth Braine, piano; William Wessel, chimes.
– "Today's Radio Program," New York Times 12-24-1924

12-24-1924 – KDKA, Pittsburgh. 8pm. *Reader:* Prof. Wayland M. Parish, Department of English, University of Pittsburgh.
– Coshocton (OH) Tribune 12-24-1924

12-24-1924 – WCAP (Wash., D.C.?) 5:30-5:45pm Pacific. *Reader:* Elizabeth Field.

12-24-1924 – WMAQ, Chicago. 9pm Central. PLAY NIGHT Cast: The WMAQ Players.
– Iowa City Press-Citizen 12-23-1924, Washington Post 12-24-1924, others.
   (*The FIRST confirmed airing of a full-cast dramatization of the* Carol.)

12-24-1924 – WLS, Chicago. 9:15-10pm. *Solo Performance?:* Wallace Bruce Amsbury. Part of a longer program.
– Seattle Daily Times 12-23-1924, Chicago Tribune 12-24-1924

12-24-1924 – WHK, Cleveland. 10pm-Early am? Central. *Reader:* Lucille A. Harding.
   "... in the air until early morning with musical and other features appropriate to the occasion... (including) Dickens' 'Christmas Carol,' which is to be read in whole or in part from at least half a dozen radio stations during their Christmas Eve

celebrations...and James Whitcomb Riley, interpretations by Burk C. Taylor."
– (Cleveland) Plain Dealer 12-24-1924

12-25-1924 – WGBS, New York. 3-4pm. *Cast:* The Triangle Players.
   "RADIO STATIONS TO FEATURE CHRISTMAS MUSIC THIS WEEK."
– New York Times 12-21-1924

12-25-1924 – KYW. 8pm. *Reader:* Rev. C. J. Pernin.
– Chicago Tribune 12-26-1924

12-19-1925 – WLW. 7:30pm. *Format?*
– Trenton Daily Times 12-12-1925

12-23-1925 – WFBH, New York. 4-4:15pm. *Format?*
– "Today's Radio Program," New York Times 12-23-1925

12-23-1925 – WLIB, Elgin, Il. 7pm Central. *Reader:* Bill Hay.
   "With musical background and musical interludes...to the accompaniment of suppressed tones from the studio organ."
– "Radio to Unite America in Christmas Observance," Chicago Tribune 12-20-1925; Elmer Douglass radio column, Chicago Tribune 12-24-1925

12-23-1925 – WNYC. 10:10-10:30pm. *Format?*
– "Today's Radio Program," New York Times 12-23-1925

12-24-1925 – KDKA. 8:15-9pm. *Reader:* Wayland M. Parish.
– Winnipeg Free Press 12-19-1925

12-24-1925 – WEAF. 11:30pm. *Reader:* Charles Howard Mills. *Music.*

12-24-1925 – WGN, Chicago. 6:30-7pm Central. *Reader:* Bill Hay.
   "Announcer Bill Hay is to continue the reading of (Dicken's Christmas Carol)."

– Chicago Tribune 12-24-1925
(*See WLIB, above; the stations were interrelated at this time.*)

12-24-1925 – WFBH. 4-4:15pm. *Format?*

12-24-1925 – KGO, Oakland, Ca. 8-9pm Pacific.
Director: Wilda Wilson Church. *Producer, Writer:* Carl Rhodehamel. *Mus.:* Arthur S. Garbett, KGO Orchestra.
   "...special radio presentation of Dickens' 'Christmas Carol.'"
– (Portland) Oregonian 12-24-1925; also Seattle Daily Times 12-24-1925

12-24-1925 – WJZ, New York. 11-11:30am. *Format?*
– "Today's Radio Program," New York Times 12-24-1925

12-24-1925 – WEAF. 11:30pm. *Reader:* Charles Howard Mills. *Mus.:* Freeda Lehmann, violinist; Mrs. C. H. Mills, pianist; William Wessell, chimes.
– "Radio Broadcasting News," Springfield (MA) Republican 12-20-1925

12-25-1925 – WEEI, Boston. 6:45pm. *Cast:* The Dramatic Club of the Big Brother Hour.
– Boston Globe 12-25-1925

12-16-1926 – WFBL, Syracuse; WGY, Schenectady; WMAK, Lockport, NY. *Cast:* Boar's Head Dramatic Society. Syracuse University program, including a *Carol*.
– Syracuse (NY) Herald 12-12-1926
   (Later *Carol*er Ernest Chappell was WFBL's announcer/station director at the time, and almost surely took part in this.)

12-16-1926 / 12-23-26 – WNYC. 5:15-5:35pm. *Reader:* Harriette Weems.
– New York Times 12-23-1926

12-23-1926 – WBZ, Springfield, Ma. 7:30-8pm. *Solo Performance:* Dr. Delbert M. Staley. *Mus.:* Colchester Ensemble.

"A dramatic impersonation of the characters in Dickens' 'Christmas Carol'"
– Hartford Courant 12-23-1926; also Springfield Republican 12-19-1926

12-24-1926 – KDKA. 7:30-8pm. *Reader:* Frederick P. Mayers.
– "Today's Radio Program," New York Times 12-24-1926, Kokomo (IN) Tribune 12-24-1926

12-24-1926 – WGN. 8pm? *Reader:* Bill Hay. *Music.*
(The *Carol* may have run from 7:30-8:30pm, followed at 10pm by "A Visit from St. Nicholas" and Bible passages.)
– Chicago Tribune 12-19-1926; on Christmas Day, the Tribune's radio columnist praised "the interpretive prose reader."

12-24-1926 – WLS. 8-9:10pm. *Reader:* Anthony Wons. *Mus.:* The Little Symphony of Chicago, George Dasch, Conductor.
– "Radio Casts a Halo Around Christmas Eve," Elmer Douglass radio column, Chicago Tribune 12-25-1926

12-24-1926 – WOR. 10:30-11:30pm. *Format?*
– Hartford Courant 12-24-26 (No other papers list this; possibly an error.)

12-24-1926 – KOA, Denver. 9:30pm Mountain. *Dir.:* Iris Ruth Gilmore.
"Professional actors …with a musical setting provided by boys' and girls' choruses, organ, chimes and instrumental trio."
– (Cleveland) Plain Dealer 12-19-1926; also Lethbridge (Alberta) Herald 12-24-1926

12-20-1927 – WNYC. 8:30-9pm. *Reader/Lecturer?:* Prof. J. G. C. Troop.
– New York Times 12-20-1927

12-22-1927 – WMES, Boston. 8:30-9pm. *Reader:* Vora Burpee.
– Boston Globe 12-22-1927

12-22-1927 – WICC, Bridgeport. 9:30-10pm. *Format?*
– "Dickens's Christmas Carols" [*sic*], New York Times 12-22-1927

12-24-1927 – WOR. 3-3:30pm. *Cast:* The Playmakers.
– New York Times 12-24-1927

12-24-1927 – WBET, Boston. 4:30-5pm. *Reader:* Prof. Charles Townsend Copeland.
"…Will read the Cratchits dinner scene from Dickens' 'Christmas Carol,' and two poems by Kipling, 'The Road to Mandalay' and 'The 'Eathen.'"
– Boston Globe 12-24-1927

12-24-1927 – KDKA. 7-7:15pm. *Reader:* Wayland M. Parish.
(Address delivered at University of Pittsburgh.)
– Lowell (MA) Sun 12-24-1927

12-24-1927 – WRNY, New York. 7:30-7:45pm. *Format?*
– New York Times 12-24-1927

12-24-1927 – WNYC. 9-9:20pm. *Format?*
"Harriette Weems, Shakespearean actress will be heard during the program beginning at 8:15 o'clock tonight over WNYC."
– New York Times 12-24-1927
(Weems' stated airtime likely due to an omnibus program containing a *Carol*.)

12-24-1927 – WGN. 8:10-9:15pm Central. *Reader:* Bill Hay. *Mus.:* W-G-N studio ensemble.
– Chicago Tribune 12-18-1927

12-24-1927 – WEAF (National Broadcasting Company Red Network). 10-10:30pm. *Solo Performance:* Chas. H. Mills. *Mus.:* violin by Arcadie Birkenholz.
– Bridgeport Telegram 12-24-1927
(*This appears to be the first documented Network broadcast of the Carol in America, beyond such small inter-station hookups as the 1926 WFBL production.*)

12-25-1927 – WRNY. 4:15-5pm. *Cast:* The Monticello Players.
– New York Times 12-25-1927

12-18-1928 – KGW, Portland. 9:30-10:30pm Pacific. *Cast. Music.*
"All the characters of the story are to appear before the microphone, and every detail has been retained in the radio version. There will be special orchestral settings, fragments of Christmas carols and other Yule sounds to add realism...."
– (Portland) Oregonian 12-18-1928

12-22-1928 – KDKA. 7-7:15pm. *Reader:* Wayland M. Parish, University of Pittsburgh
– Olean (NY) Times 12-22-1928

12-22-1928 – WGN. 8-9pm Central. *Dir.:* Harry W. Spingold. *Cast:* The W-G-N Players.
– Chicago Tribune 12-22-1928

12-22-1928 – WJZ; NBC, Inc. West Coast. 10:15-11pm. GOLDEN LEGENDS. *Dir.:* Ted Maxwell. *Cast:* The National Players.
– Christian Science Monitor 12-18-1928

12-24-1928 – WOR; WMAL, Wash., D.C.; WADC, Akron; WHK; WKRC, Cincinnati; WSPD, Toledo; other Columbia Broadcasting System stations. 10pm-12am. *Cast. Music.*
"A two-hour radio... full dramatization, with incidental music to accompany it."
– Hartford Courant 12-23-1928, and others.
"The principal feature on the schedule of the Columbia Broadcasting System of 20 stations, headed by WOR... followed at midnight... by a program of Christmas carols by a mixed chorus."
– Centralia (WA) Daily Chronicle 12-24-1928; also Hamilton (OH) Daily News 12-24-1928

12-24-1928 – WLS. *Cast:* Scrooge, Tony Wons.
"Anthony Wand, [*sic*] poet, played the part of Scrooge, and played it perfectly."

– "Listening In" column, Decatur (WA) Review 12-25-1928

12-15-1929 – WJR, Pontiac, Mich. 6pm. *Cast:* The WJR Players.
– Sandusky (OH) Register 12-15-1929

12-23-1929 – WOR. 7-7:30pm. *Reader:* E. Livingston Barbour.
– New York Times 12-23-1929

12-23-1929 – WGN. 9-10pm Central. *Dir.:* Harry W. Spingold. *Wr.:* Jean Conover. *Mus.:* St. Chrysostom's Choir, W-G-N Orchestra. *Cast:* The WGN Players.
– Chicago Tribune 12-23-1929

12-24-1929 – WEAF, NBC stations. 7-7:30pm. SOCONYLAND SKETCHES *Cast:* Scrooge, Arthur Allen; Parker Fennelly; more?
– "YULETIDE MUSIC VIBRATES THE AIR," New York Times 12-22-1929; Hartford Courant 12-24-1929

12-24-1929 – WABC, W2XE (shortwave) New York; CBS stations. 11pm-12am. *Prd./Dir./Wr.:* Don Clark, Georgia Backus, Julius Seebach. *Mus.:* Howard Barlow & Columbia Symphony Orchestra. *Cast:* Scrooge, Jack Soanes; Narrator, David Ross; Tiny Tim, Donald Hughes; Bob Cratchit, Allyn Joslyn; Mrs. Cratchit, Marie Gerard; Marley's Ghost, Reynolds Evans; Martha, Helen Nugent; Tom, Mark Hawley; Fred, Don Bell; Spirit of Christmas Past, Brad Sutton; Spirit of Christmas Present, Vere Johns; Spirit of Christmas Yet to Come, Mark Loebell; Virgil, Harriet Lee; Gentleman, Claude Archer; Announcer, Frank Knight.
  (Jamaican's Vere Johns was one of the first persons of color to act on American network radio, and his work here is well covered in The [Jamaica] Gleaner of 12-23-1929, 12-30-1929, and 1-14-1930) Also see The Milwaukee Journal 12-22-1929.

12-19-1930 – WEAO, Columbus, Oh. 3:30pm. *Cast:* Ohio State Players.
  "...hear ... Dickens' 'A Christmas Carol,' a drama you'll hear frequently now that the holidays are here."
– (Cleveland) Plain Dealer 12-19-1930

12-23-1930 – WEAF, NBC stations. 7:30pm. SOCONYLAND SKETCHES *Wr.*, Henry Fiske, William Ford Manley. *Cast:* Scrooge, Arthur Allen; Soconyland Players.
"...the exclusive presentation, on the National Broadcasting Company networks...of...'The [sic] Christmas Carol....'"
– Kingston Daily Freeman 12-16-1930; New York Times 12-21-1930

12-23-1930 – WGN. 8-9pm. *Reader:* Rev. John Evans (Religion Editor, Chicago Tribune).
"...first installment...tomorrow night at 10:10 the story will be continued."
– Chicago Tribune 12-23-1930

12-24-1930 – WABC; WRDC, Hartford; other CBS stations. 11pm-12am. *Prd., Dir., Wr.:* Georgia Backus, Don Clark. *Mus.:* Howard Barlow, w/Orchestra, Chorus. *Cast:* Scrooge, Jack Soanes; Tiny Tim, Donald Hughes; Narr., David Ross; more.
– Hartford Courant 12-21-1930

12-24-1930 – WAIU, Columbus, Oh. Pm. *Reader:* Dr. Delbert G. Lean (Oratory Department head, College of Wooster).
"(Lean) will give (the Carol) over WAIU...it was announced today. (Also) this season, the 23d consecutive year Dr. Lean has read the Carol in Memorial Chapel, he will deliver it the evening of Dec. 18, the night before Christmas recess starts."
– (Cleveland) Plain Dealer 12-03-1930

12-23-1931 – WJZ; NBC stations. 9-9:30pm. *Wr.:* Edith Meiser. *Cast:* Scrooge, Richard Gordon; Narr., Leigh Lovell.
– "Today on the Radio," New York Times 12-23-1931
 (In the usual *Sherlock Holmes* slot, with that series' stars.)

12-24-1931 – WABC; CBS stations. 11pm-12am. *Mus.:* Howard Barlow, w/Orchestra, Chorus. *Cast:* Scrooge, Robert Vivian; Tiny Tim, Donald Hughes.
"On the stroke of midnight, as the Dickens sketch ends ... an hour's program of carol music."

– "CHRISTMAS ON THE AIR," New York Times 12-20-1931

12-24-1931 – KFWB, Los Angeles. 9-9:30pm Pacific.
"As for Christmas plays... Dickens's [sic] 'Christmas Carol' is the masterpiece on KFWB's schedule...."
– "RADIO TO ECHO JOYOUS NOTE," Los Angeles Times 12-24-1931

12-??-1931 – NBC Syndication? (40 min.) *Prd.:* George P. Ludlam?
(*There is a recording in circulation sometimes indentified with this time and origination, but this is unconfirmed. See note in the body of this book where that era is covered.*)

12-25-1931 – WOR. 2-2:30pm. *Solo Performer?:* Frank Speaight.
– New York Times 12-25-1931; Hartford Courant 12-25-1931

12-25-1931 – WLWL, New York. 6:45pm.

12-26-1931 – WGBS. 1-1:30pm. *Cast:* Damroth Players.
– "Today on the Radio," New York Times 12-26-1931

12-24-1932 – WJZ and NBC. 9:30-10pm. *Cast:* Scrooge, Tom Terris.
"...famous (Scrooge)...."
– Washington Post 12-18-1932; New York Times 12-24-1932

12-24-1932 – WABC and CBS. 10-11pm. *Wr.:* Don Clark. *Mus.:* Howard Barlow, Orchestra.
– Washington Post 12-18-1932

12-24-1933 – WABC and CBS. 11-12pm.
"...dramatized with Alexander Woollcott as narrator. The Barlow Orchestra will contribute the musical background."
– "YULETIDE ON THE AIR," – New York Times 12-24-1933
(Also see especially "A LISTENER'S CRITICISM – Harold F. Loekle," New York Times 12-31-1933.)

12-25-1934 – CBS. 2:30am-5:15pm. CHRISTMAS PARTY
Sponsor: The Nash Motor Company. *Cast (of PARTY):* From Chicago – M.C., Alexander Woollcott; Beatrice Lillie, Victor Young, Madame Ernestine Schumann-Heink, Kathryn Witwer, George Olsen Orchestra, Ethel Shutta, Apollo Club Chorus. From New York – Don Cossack's Russian Male Chorus. From Los Angeles (KHJ) – Barrymore and *Carol* cast.
– NY Eve. Post 11-23-1934; also Washington Post 12-25-1934
   (*Lionel Barrymore's broadcast debut, and his historic first portrayal of Ebenezer Scrooge. Likely a 60 min. Carol, as were CBS's immediately before and after this one.*)

12-25-1935 – CBS. 5-5:30pm. *Spons.:* Campbell's Soup. *Cast:* Scrooge, Lionel Barrymore; Tiny Tim, Buster Phelps.
– NewYork Herald Tribune 12-22-1935; also New York American 12-23-1935
   (The 12/28/1935 Saturday Evening Post has a full page, full color ad for this broadcast on p.25.)

12-25-1936 – CBS. 9-10pm. HOLLYWOOD HOTEL
Spons.: Campbell's Soups. *Cast:* Hostess, Louella Parsons; M.C., Dick Powell; Scrooge, *John* Barrymore.
   (*Lionel Barrymore's ailing wife died the day before the broadcast, and his brother John took his place at the mike.*)
– New York Times 12-20-1936; also, Washington Post 12-26-1936; Saturday Evening Post 12-26-1936 has a full page, full color ad for the broadcast on p.27.)

12-??-1936 – BBC. *Wr.:* Philip Wade.

12-25-1937 – CBS. 4-5:45pm. HOLLYWOOD HOTEL
Spons.: Campbell's Soups. *Cast:* Scrooge, Lionel Barrymore.
   "...Tommy Kelly and Jackie Moran... preview of 'Tom Sawyer,' followed by Lionel Barrymore in 'A Christmas Carol.'"
– Chicago Tribune 12-25-1937
   (Tom Sawyer segment, 60m.; The *Carol*, 45m.)

12-25-1937 – Synd.? (29 min.) RCA/NBC THESAURUS?

Cast: (Per William Nadel audit:) Scrooge, Ted Osborne; Charity Collector & Christmas Past, Howard McNear; (Per Craig Wichman audit:) Bob Cratchit, Joe Kearns; Fred, Hans Conried; Christmas Present, Gavin Gordon; Ancr., Truman Bradley?

(*There is a recording in circulation sometimes indentified with this time and origination, but those details are unconfirmed; see note in the body of this book where that era is covered. Also, a re-edited version of this production was syndicated by C.P. MacGregor in 1950.*)

12-15-1938 – NBC. 9-10pm. (Maxwell House Coffee presents) GOOD NEWS OF 1939 *Mus.:* Meredith Wilson. *Cast:* Ancr., Warren Hull; MC, Robert Young; Frank Morgan, Fanny Brice, Hanley Stafford, Tony Martin.

Includes a 20 min. Carol: Dir.: Edwin L. Marin. *Mus.:* Franz Waxman. *Cast:* Narr., Lionel Barrymore; Scrooge, Reginald Owen; Bob Cratchit, Gene Lockhart; Mrs. Cratchit, Kathleen Lockhart; Young Scrooge, Ronald Sinclair; Christmas Past, Ann Rutherford.

(Lionel Barrymore replaced by Reginald Owen in the lead. See note in the body of this book where that era is covered.)

12-23-1938 – CBS. 9-10pm. THE CAMPBELL PLAYHOUSE *Prd., Dir.:* Orson Welles. *Wr.:* Howard Koch. *Mus.:* Bernard Herrmann. *Sound Effects:* Ora Nichols. *Cast:* Narr. & Scrooge, Orson Welles (sub. for Lionel Barrymore); Nephew Fred, Joseph Cotten; Bob Cratchit, Hiram Sherman; Charity Gent, Ray Collins; Tiny Tim, Kingsley Colton; Belle's Husband, Edgar Barrier; Ghost of Christmas Present, Eustace Wyatt; Ghost of Christmas Yet To Come, Frank Readick; Marley's Ghost, Alfred Shirley; Charwoman, Alice Frost; Ghost of Christmas Past, Arthur Anderson; Mr. Fezziwig, George Spelvin; Mrs. Cratchit, Brenda Forbes; Belle, Anna Stafford; Bill Herz (bit part, per radio historian William Nadel); Announcer, Earnest Chappell.

(Arthur Anderson would recreate his role in this script before a live and broadcast audience 72 years later. See the 12-24-2010 WWNC production below.)

12-19-1939 – WRNL, Richmond. 3:30-4pm. *Prd., Dir.:* Althea Hunt, Tom Forsyth. *Music. Cast:* The William and Mary (College) Players.
   "'Christmas Carol' will be performed...tomorrow afternoon on the stage of Phi Beta Kappa Memorial Hall.... The program will be open to the public, and will give local residents a chance to see how a radio play is made up and presented."
– Richmond (VA) Newsleader 12-18-1939

12-24-1939 – Mutual Broadcasting System. 2:45-3:30pm. *Spons.:* Chicago Tribune. *Cast:* Scrooge, Hugh Studebaker; Olan Soule, Willard Waterman. (Produced at WGN, Chicago.)
– Chicago Tribune 12-24-1939

12-24-1939 – CBS. 8-9pm. THE CAMPBELL PLAYHOUSE *Prd., Dir.:* Orson Welles. *Mus.:* Bernard Herrmann. *Sfx.:* Harry Essman, Cliff Thorson. *Cast:* Scrooge, Lionel Barrymore; Host & Narr., Orson Welles; Marley & Young Scrooge, Everett Sloane; Christmas Past, Edgar Barrier; Christmas Present & Second Gent on Street, George Coulouris; Charity Gent & Fezziwig, Ray Collins; Belle, Georgia Backus; Mrs. Cratchit, Bea Benaderet; Bob Cratchit, Frank Readick; Erskine Sanford; Ancr., Ernest Chappell.
– Charleston (WV) Daily Mail 12-24-1939
   (*Best known of all network radio productions of the Carol, and of the eighteen total broadcasts featuring Lionel Barrymore as Scrooge, likely one of only three, along with 1935's and his 1934 debut, that were a full hour in length.*)

12-20-1940 – CBS. 9:30-10pm. THE CAMPBELL PLAYHOUSE Scrooge, Lionel Barrymore.
– Variety New York 12-18-1940; Variety Los Angeles 12-25-1940; also Wisconsin State Journal 12-15-1940

1941 – **DECCA RECORDS**. 78 rpm. (25 min.) Recorded Sept. 17, 1941; released in November. *Prd., Dir.:* George Wells. *Mus. Dir.:* Victor Young. *Vocal Dir.:* Ken Darby. *Cast:* Ebenezer Scrooge, Ronald Colman; Bob Cratchit, Eric Snowden; Tiny Tim, Barbara Jean Wong; Jacob Marley, Lou Merrill; First Ghost, Hans

Conried; Second Ghost, Cy Kendall: Third Ghost, Gale Gordon; Mrs. Cratchit, Heather Thatcher; Fred (Nephew), Fred Mackaye; Boy, Stephen Muller; Belle (Sweetheart), Duane Thompson; Mr. Portly, Ferdinand Munier; Men In Street, Gale Gordon & Fred Mackaye.

(The later LP reissue omits the charity collectors scene, still unrestored on the current CD.)

1941 – (RCA) VICTOR RECORDS. 78 rpm. (40 min.) *Prd., Wr., Narr.:* Ernest Chappell. *Mus.:* Lew White; Quartet: Mary Merker, Soprano; Paula Heminghous, Contralto; Henry Shope, Tenor; Walter Preston, Baritone. *Sfx.:* Charles Range. *Cast:* Scrooge, Eustace Wyatt; Bob Cratchit, John McGovern; Marley's Ghost & Belle's Husband, John Gibson; Ghost of Christmas Past, Richard Gordon; Ghost of Christmas Present, Shirling Oliver; Nephew Fred, Bud Collier [*sic*]; The Solicitor, Craig McDonnell; Mrs. Cratchit, Helen Brown; Tiny Tim, Larry Robinson; Martha Cratchit, Evelyn Devine; Master Peter Cratchit, Dickie Van Patton; Belinda Cratchit & Belle, Leslie Woods; Two Men on the Street, Alfred Shirley & Burford Hampden; Boy on the Street, James Donnolly.

"Dickens 'Christmas Carol' Tops Children's Yuletide Albums" – Jay Walz, Washington Post 11-16-1941

(See main body of book for the story of the novel use of this record by WJTN's J. Ralph Carlson.)

12-22/26-1941 – WOR, & Mutual Broadcasting System. 4:15-4:30pm. (Five Part Serial.) Cast: Scrooge, Edmund Gwenn; Tiny Tim, Ted Donaldson.

12-23-1941 – MBS/Don Lee Network. 3-3:30pm. THE DON LEE HOLLYWOOD PLAYHOUSE?
Dir.,: Ed Robinson. *Wr., Solo Performer?:* Donald Chapman. *Mus:* Organ, Skitch Henderson. Ancr., David Young.
– Los Angeles Times listing 12-23-41

12-25-1941 – NBC. 10-10:30pm. THE RUDY VALLEE SHOW
Spons.: Sealtest. *Cast:* Host & Narr., Rudy Vallee; Scrooge, Lionel

Barrymore; Mrs. Cratchit, Kathleen Lockhart; Anne Stone, Barbara Jean Wong; Martha, June Lockhart; Marley & Young Scrooge, Hans Conried; Eric Snowden, Byron Kane, Tommy Barnes, Lou Merrill, Dix Davis.

1942 – BBC. *Prd.;* John Burrell. *Wr.:* Max Kester.

1942 – **COLUMBIA RECORDS**, M-MM-521. 78 rpm. (23 min. 43 sec.) Recorded July 26, 1942. *Prd., Dir.:* Tom McNight. *Wr.:* Edith Meiser (Mrs. McKnight). *Mus.:* Leith Stevens. *Cast:* Scrooge, Basil Rathbone; Fred, Elliot Lewis; Bob Cratchet [*sic*], Jay Novello; Portly Man & 1ST Man, Arthur Q. Bryan; Marley's Ghost & Undertaker's Man, Raymond Lawrence; Christmas Past, Francis X. Bushman; Scrooge as a Boy & Tiny Tim, Tommy Cook; Little Fan, Rhoda Williams; Christmas Present & 2ND Man, Stuart Robertson; Mrs. Cratchet & Charwoman, Paula Winslowe; Peter, Dix Davis; Martha, Lurene Tuttle; Boy, Walter Tetley; Narr., Harlow Wilcox.

12-24-1942 – NBC. 10-10:30pm. VALLEE VARIETIES (THE RUDY VALLEE SHOW) *Spons.:* Sealtest. *Cast:* Host, Rudy Vallee; Scrooge, Lionel Barrymore; Cratchit Boy (?), Dix Davis

12-24-1942 – WGES, Chicago. 8-10pm Central. Paul Saltimieras. (In Lithuanian.)
– Chicago Tribune 12-24-1942

12-24-1942 – WIND, Chicago. 11:05-11:30pm Central. *Cast:* Scrooge, Basil Rathbone. "…set to music by… Leith Stevens."
– Chicago Tribune 12-24-1942
    (The same Scrooge and musical director of the then-new Columbia Records *Carol*, and of the proper length; possibly a broadcast of same?)

12-25-1942 – Synd. (15 min.) TREASURY STAR PARADE "A MODERN SCROOGE" *Prd., Dir.:* William A. Bacher. *Wr.:* Noah Huston, Joseph Roscoe. *Mus.:* David Broekman, Orchestra & Chorus. *Cast:* Host, Fredric March; Jeb Kreaker, Lionel

Barrymore; J. Donald Wilson; Announcers, Paul Douglas & Larry Elliot.
– Chicago Tribune 12-25-42

12-22-1943 – CBS. 9-9:30pm. MAYOR OF THE TOWN
Wr.: Jean Holloway? *Cast:* Scrooge, Lionel Barrymore; Marley, Hans Conried; Mrs. Cratchit, Agnes Moorehead; Announcer/Narrator, Frank Martin?
(*There is an Armed Forces Radio Service recording in circulation sometimes indentified with this time and origination, but in the present author's opinion this date is probably incorrect. See note in the body of this book where that era is covered.*)

12-24/25-1943? – NBC. CHRISTMAS AT THE FRONT? (Special shortwave broadcast to troops overseas.) *Cast:* Scrooge, Basil Rathbone; Cynthia Rathbone
(See http://www.basilrathbone.net; see also Basil Rathbone autobiography, *In and Out of Character*. The details of the broadcast described above are unconfirmed; it may be another performance of, or a misdating of, the production listed below.)

12-25-1943 – CBS. 12:30-1pm. STARS OVER HOLLYWOOD
Cast: Scrooge, Basil Rathbone. Orchestra & Chorus.
– Ad, New York Times 12-25-1943

12-25-1943 – WRC, Wash., D.C. 1-2pm.

(*Lionel Barrymore is named "Best Actor of 1942-1943" in a poll of national radio listeners, based largely his annual* Carols *and the* MAYOR *series.*)

12-23-1944 – CBS. 7-7:30pm. MAYOR OF THE TOWN
Wr.: Jean Holloway? *Cast:* Scrooge, Lionel Barrymore; Mrs. Cratchit, Agnes Moorehead; Christmas Past, Joe Kearns?
– LIFE magazine, 12-25-1944; text with 7-page photo section of Barrymore in fully cast and staged Carol scenes.
(*As with the 1943 Mayor Carol above, there is an Armed Forces Radio Service [Globe Theater] recording in circulation sometimes*

indentified with this time and origination, but the date is unconfirmed. See note in the body of this book where that era is covered.)

12-24-1944 – WOR, New York, WOL, Wash. D.C., other Mutual stations? 10:15-10:45pm. *Dir.?, Wr., Narr.:* Ernest Chappell, *Cast:* Scrooge, Everett Sloane.
– Radio pages, Washington Post 12-24-1944

12-25-1944 – WABC (CBS). *Spons.:* Dari-Rich. 3:30-4pm. *Cast:* Scrooge, Basil Rathbone.

12-22-1945 – CBS. 8:30-9pm. MAYOR OF THE TOWN
Wr.: Jean Holloway? *Cast:* Scrooge, Lionel Barrymore; Agnes Moorehead.
– Wisconsin State Journal 12-22-1945

12-21-1946 – CBS. 8:30-9pm. MAYOR OF THE TOWN
Wr.: Jean Holloway? *Cast:* Scrooge, Lionel Barrymore; Mrs. Cratchit, Agnes Moorehead; Announcer, Ken Peters?
– Associated Press, Charleston (WV) Daily Mail 12-21-1946

12-24-1947 – ABC. 8:30-9pm. MAYOR OF THE TOWN
Wr.: Jean Holloway? *Cast:* Scrooge, Lionel Barrymore.
– Racine (WIS) Journal-Times 12-24-1947

1947 – **MGM Records**, MGM-16. 78 rpm. (24 min.) *Dir., Wr.:* Dailey Paskman. *Mus.:* Sammy Timberg. *Cast:* Scrooge, Lionel Barrymore; Narrator, Richard Hale; Fred, Ben Wright?; Marley, Henry Daniell ? (Author's guess.)
RELEASE HISTORY:
1947: MGM-16 (4 x 10" 78 rpm)
1950: MGM-16 (78 rpm)
      MGM E-520 (10" 33 1/3 LP)
1953: MGM X-16 (2 x 45 rpm EP)
195?: MGM K-16A (4 x 45 rpm)
1955: MGM E-3222 (12" LP; music, Canterbury Choir)
1959: Lion L70124 (LP; Canterbury) (Lion was MGM's budget children's label.)

1962: MGM CH-112 (LP; Canterbury)
196?: Longines Symphonette/MGM LW-116 (LP; music, David Rose)
1965: MGM PM-20 (LP; Canterbury)
1966: MGM PMS-32 (LP; Canterbury; simulated Stereo)
1970: MGM SE-4746 (LP; Canterbury; sim. Stereo)
1995: Umvd Special Markets/Polygram (CD; Canterbury)
2010: Guideposts (3-CD, "All-Time Greatest Hits of Christmas")

12-23-47? – Armed Forces Radio Service. (25 min.) GLOBE THEATER. Host, Herbert Marshall; Narr., Frank Martin.
  (Repackaging of a MAYOR OF THE TOWN *Carol*, perhaps 1944's—see note for that program above.)

12-25-1948 – WWDC (Wash., D.C.). 12-1pm.

12-25-1948 – WAIT (Chicago). 11-11:15am.

12-25-1948 – CBS. *Spons.:* Wrigley's. 4pm-6pm. CHRISTMAS FESTIVAL
Cast: Gene Autry, Danny Kaye, John Nesbitt telling "The Juggler of Notre Dame"; Burns and Allen, Sweeney and March, Hedda Hopper, The Andrews Sisters, Lise Roy and Jacques Normand, Eddie "Rochester" Anderson, Walter Gross, Mitchell Boys' choir. *Including a Carol of unknown length. Cast:* Scrooge, Lionel Barrymore.

12-25-1948 – KYDL (NBC, Salt Lake City.)
  (May have aired the Barrymore 1947 MGM Record?)

1949 – **REGAL RECORD CORP.** "Tots 'N' Teens" 3" x 7" 78RPM. (3 min. 16 sec.) *Solo Performance:* Ireene Wicker, "The Singing Lady." (This appears to the first specifically "Kiddie Record" production of the *Carol*.)

12-25-1949? – Synd. (26 min.) TOWERS OF LONDON (British) *Cast:* Scrooge, John Mills; Alec Guinness; Margaret Lockwood; Dirk Bogarde; Guy Roth; Jean Simmons; Googie Withers; John McCallum; Derek Bond. (J. Arthur Rank Organization actors.)

12-24-1949 – Synd. FAVORITE STORY.
Cast: Scrooge, Ronald Colman; Christmas Future, Joseph Kearns; Fred, Jimmy Lydon; Charity Gent, Arthur Q. Bryan; John Beals, Lurene Tuttle; Henry Blair, Eric Snowden, Jerry Farber, Cyrus Kendall, Earl Leeds.
(From the same script as Colman's 1941 record.)

1949 – **DECCA RECORDS.** (4 x 45 rpm.)
(Reissue of Colman's 1941 78 rpm production).

12-24-1949 – CBS. 1-1:30pm. STARS OVER HOLLYWOOD
Cast: Scrooge, (and Charles Dickens?), Edmund Gwenn.
(The first of several turns in the role by Gwenn on this series. In the recordings of his 1951 and 1953 STARS Carols, Gwenn doubles as the author; it is likely he did so in all of them.)

12-25-1949 – MBS. 2:30-3:30pm. CAPEHEART CHRISTMAS HOUR
Prd., Dir.: Dick Mack. *Mus.:* Lyn Murray. *Cast:* Scrooge, Lionel Barrymore; Narr., Bill Johnstone; Eric Snowden, Byron Kane, Joseph Kearns, Sonny Barnett, Shirley Mitchell, Shepard Menken, Sylvia Syms, Jeffrey Silver, Mala Powers.
(The *Carol*, plus 30 min. of music.)

12-22-1950 – MBS. (30 min.) HOLLYWOOD THEATER (OF STARS)
Prd., Host, Narr.: C.P. MacGregor. *Cast:* (Per William Nadel audit:) Scrooge, Ted Osborne; Christmas Past, Howard McNear; (Per Craig Wichman audit:) Bob Cratchit, Joe Kearns; Christmas Present, Gavin Gordon.
(MacGregor was a prolific producer of syndicated radio for several decades. This program likely ran in other venues at other times as well; one source indicates an NBC airing of this series. A recording is extant with framing passages by MacGregor from 1950— or perhaps even later—but the actual *Carol* is a re-edit of the production that circulates labeled as a 1937 NBC Thesaurus show.)

12-24-1950 – MBS. 4-4:30pm.

Spons.: A.O. Smith. *Prd., Dir.,:* Dick Mack. *Mus.:* Lynn Murray. *Cast:* Scrooge, Lionel Barrymore; Narrator, Gerald Mohr; Mala Powers, Joseph Kearns, Eric Snowden, Betty Lou Gerson, Byron Kane, Shirley Mitchell, Shepard Menken, Jeffrey Silver, Sonny Barnett, Sammy Ogg, Larry Chatterton; Announcer, Larry Jasden (sp?)

12-22-1951 – CBS. 12:30-1pm. STARS OVER HOLLYWOOD
Dir.: Hans Conried. *Wr.:* Ralph Rose. *Mus.:* Rex Koury. *Cast:* Scrooge, Edmund Gwenn; Betty Harford, Ben Wright, Eric Snowden, Jay Novello, Raymond Lawrence, Charlie Lung, Tudor Owen, Diane Abbott; Host, Art Ballinger.

12-23-1951 – MBS. 4-4:30pm.
Spons.: A.O. Smith. *Cast:* Scrooge, Lionel Barrymore.

12-25-1951 – WQXR, New York. (BBC Syndication). 4:30-5pm.
Prd.: Cleland Finn. *Mus.:* Harold Evans; *Cond.:* Trevor Harvey. *Cast:* Scrooge, Alec Guiness; Brian Poney, Charles Leno, Denise Briar, Ella Milm, Gabriel Blunt, Hamilton Dyce, Jeffrey Underwood, John Charlesworth, Leslie Crowder, Martin Lewis, Michael Harding, Stanley Groom, Susan Richards; Narrator, Keith Pyatt.
(*Some sources say that this program was actually produced in 1950.*)

1951 – **RCA VICTOR RECORDS**. 78 rpm Y-440, 45 rpm WY-440, 33 rpm PRM184. (15 min. 7 sec.) Inc. Story Booklet. *Prd.:* Steven R. Carlin. *Wr.:* Martin Weldon. *Mus.:* Comp. & Cond. by Frank Worth, w/Orchestra. *Cast:* Narrator, Charles Laughton; Scrooge, William D. Cottrell; Fred, William Phipps; Bob Cratchit, Harry LeRoy Burnett; Marley's Ghost, Victor H. Perrin.
("New release," per Billboard magazine 10-6-1951)

12-20-1952 – CBS. 12:30-1pm. STARS OVER HOLLYWOOD
Cast: Scrooge, Edmund Gwenn.

12-21-1952 – CBS. 9-9:30pm. HALLMARK PLAYHOUSE
Cast: Scrooge, Lionel Barrymore.

1953? – **CRICKET RECORDS**, CX-8 (45 rpm, 33 1/3 rpm, 78 rpm?) *Reader?:* Brett Morrison
(Later reissued on LP with several Christmas songs.)

12-19-1953 – CBS. 12:30-1pm. STARS OVER HOLLYWOOD
Dir.: Don Clark. *Cast:* Scrooge, Edmund Gwenn; Gigi Pearson, Bill Johnstone, Victor Perrin, Eric Snowden, Raymond Lawrence, Parley Baer; Tiny Tim, Lonnie Burr; Host, Art Ballinger.

12-20-1953 – CBS. 9-9:30pm. HALLMARK HALL OF FAME
Prd., Dir.: William Froug. *Wr.:* Leonard St. Clair. *Cast:* Scrooge, Lionel Barrymore; Narrator, John Stephenson; Mrs. Cratchit, Virginia Gregg; Martha, Anne Whitfield; Byron Kane; Fred, Lamont Johnson; Herb Butterfield, Christmas Past?, Parley Baer; Marley?, Joseph Kearns; Ted De Corsia, Lawrence Dobkin; Turkey Boy, Richard Beals; Tiny Tim, Stuffy Singer; Announcer, Frank Goss.
(*The LAST of Lionel Barrymore's 18 original broadcast portrayals of Ebenezer Scrooge in Charles Dickens'* A Christmas Carol.)
BROADCAST HISTORY – Lionel Barrymore on the air as Ebenezer Scrooge:
1934 - #1
1935 - #2
1936 - (John Barrymore)
1937 - #3
1938 - (Reginald Owen / Orson Welles)
1939 - #4
1940 - #5
1941 - #6
1942 - #7
1943 - #8
1944 - #9
1945 - #10
1946 - #11
1947 - #12
1948 - #13
1949 - #14
1950 - #15
1951 - #16

1952 - #17
1953 - #18
(Total is 19 if counting the 1947 MGM record, which was broadcast several times.)

12-22-1953 – CKLW, Detroit. (60 min.) *Spons.:* Philco of Michigan. *Prd:* Art Sutton. *Cast:* Rick Roberts ork, Joe Gentile. *Musicians:* Ruth Fraser, violin; George Dorn, tenor; Genevieve Atwood, contralto; Radian Singers.
– Variety 12-30-1953

12-24-1953 – WVNJ, Newark, N.J.. 9-10pm. The 1941 Ronald Colman *Carol.* Also, music by the Rutgers Glee Club.
– Westfield (NJ) Leader 12-24-1953

12-24-1953, 12-25-53 – WCFM, Wash. D.C. (45 min.) *Dir.:* Denis E. Connell. *Tech. Prd.:* Harold Schangagel. *Cast:* Washington Chapel Players: Scrooge, George Farrington; Charles Dickens, Gordon Wallace; Bob Cratchit, Paul W. Murphy; Narr., Bess Davis Schreiner; Adele Whiteside, Lansing Hall, Others.
– Variety 12-30-1953

12-24-1953 – NBC. THEATRE ROYAL
Prd., Dir.: Harry Alan Towers. *Wr.:* Derek Patmore. *Mus.:* Sidney Torch. *Cast:* Narrator & Scrooge, Laurence Olivier; Peter Bull? (Author's guess.)
 (A slightly trimmed edit of this production has seen several LP and CD releases through the years.)

11-1954 – **CAMDEN (RCA) RECORDS**, CAL-137. LP reissue of 1941 Victor 78 rpm set.
 (*Unfortunately, this seems to be the only rerelease ever of this excellent Chappell CAROL.*)

12-19-1954 – CBS. 6:30-7pm. HALLMARK HALL OF FAME
Host, Edward Arnold.
 (*Lionel Barrymore had died at age 76 on November 16th, so his 1953 production was rebroadcast as a tribute.*)

12-25-1954 – WABC. 8:30-9pm.
Cast: Alec Guiness. (Rebroadcast of 1951 show.)

10-28-1955 – **MGM Records**, #E3222. 33 1/3 LP reissue of Barrymore's 1947 78 rpm set.
– "New Releases from MGM Records," Fall 1955

12-24-1955 – MBS/WOR. 7:30-8pm.
Cast: Scrooge, Lionel Barrymore.
   (*A rebroadcast of one of Barrymore's 1949-1951 MBS shows, or of his 1947 MGM record.*)

12-24-1955 – WINS. 8-8:30pm.
Cast: Scrooge, Basil Rathbone. (Possibly an airing of one of his 1940's broadcasts or his 1942 record.)

12-25-1955 – WABC. 12-12:30pm.
Cast: Alec Guiness. (Rebroadcast of his 1951 show.)

1955? – **GOLDEN RECORDS**, R261. 78 rpm & 45 rpm. (3 min. 20 sec.) "Howdy Doody – A Christmas Carol." Spoken and Sung. *Wr., Mus.:* Mary Rodgers Beaty. *Orch. & Chor. Dir.:* Mitch Miller. *Cast:* Narrator, Bob Smith; Scrooge, Captain Scuttlebutt (Allen Swift?); Bob Cratchit, Howdy Doody (Bob Smith); Tiny Tim, Dilly Dally (Bill LeCornec?).

(*In the decade between 1955 and 1965, several stations aired either the 1947 record with Lionel Barrymore, or one of Ronald Colman's Carols, either his 1941 record or 1949 broadcast.*)

12-22-1957 – CBS. 6:30-6:55pm. *Spons.:* Pennick & Ford, Ltd., Inc. *Cast:* Scrooge, Lionel Barrymore. Host, Sir Cedric Hardwicke.
– Per CBS Radio press release.
   (According to the article an in the Tuscaloosa News of 12-20-1957, this appears to have been a broadcast of the 1947 MGM records production.)

1959 – **ARGO/SPOKEN ARTS RECORDS**; also WESTMIN-STER, 728. LP. *Dir.:* Arthur Luce Klein. *Solo Performance:* Frank Pettingell. *Music.*

"Surprisingly this is the first Christmas Carol on LP, although Bransby Williams is billed as Scrooge in a Dickens miscellany. Frank Pettingell has been a stalwart of the English stage for the best part of half a century, and ever a Dickensian. This is indeed a rather maudlin tale, but it is saved from going over the edge by the author's genius for local colour and by certain opportunities which any competent narrator (Dickens included) could seize. Mr. Pettingell will not disappoint either his or the story's admirers, and it only remains to say that the cuts are well arranged and the tale moves forward naturally to its touching close."
– R.W., Gramaphone magazine 12-1959

(R.W. was either unaware of the previous Colman, Wyatt, Rathbone, Barrymore, McKenna, and O'Herlihy record versions of the tale, or discounted some of them because they did not originate on LP. Some sources cite 1956 as the date of origination for this production, but that may just be the date of the Spoken Arts label's debut.)

1959 – **TOP RANK/VANGUARD RECORDS**, 35/015. *Wr.:* Dominick Roche. *Mus.:* inc. Mutel Library cues. *Cast:* Spirits of Christmas Past, Present, and To Come – Siobhan McKenna; Scrooge, Anew McMaster; Dominick Roche, Vincent Dowling, Cecil Barror, Brenda Doyle, Coralie Carmichael, Milo O'Shea, Eve Watkinson, Ronnie Walsh.
– Hugh Mulligan, AP Newsfeatures 12-14-1960

1959? – **AUDIO BOOK CO.**. "A Talking Book," GL-614; also Listening Library, A 1634. (184 min.) *Reader:* Dan O'Herlihy.

(*The FIRST uncut recording of Dickens' text, on four 16 2/3 rpm discs. Some sources claim a 1956 origination for this recording; but the Library of Congress copyright notation says 1959.*)

1960s (Early?) – BBC. (30 min.) THE KEN DODD SHOW (Parody.)

1960 – **EMI RECORDS** / Classics For Pleasure, CFP 180. *Mus.:* The Jacques Orchestra, *Cond.:* David Willcocks. *Cast:* Narrator & Scrooge, Bernard Miles; 1st Gentleman & Ghost Of Christmas Past, Anthony Jacobs; 2nd Gentleman & Marley's Ghost, Harold Berens; Clerk Cratchit, George Rougicek; Fezziwig & Ghost Of Christmas Present, Derek Francis; Mrs. Cratchit, Barbara Hicks; Tiny Tim, Nicholas Clay; Young Cratchits, Nigel Clay & Rachel Clay; The Bach Choir.

1960 – **MERCURY/CHILDCRAFT RECORDS,** EP-C-26. 78 rpm, 33 rpm, 45 rpm. *Solo Performance:* Claude Rains, as Scrooge. *Mus.:* Hugo Peretti Orchestra, and The Caroleers. (The 33 1/3 contains other performers' back catalogue recordings; the 45 EP-C-265 the *Carol* plus "The Christmas Tree"; and 78 #53, the *Carol* alone.)
– Billboard 10-17-1960, 11-7-1960

1960 – **CAEDMON RECORDS**, TC 1135/Stereo. LP; later Reel-to-Reel and CD. *Dir.:* Howard Sackler. *Cast:* The Author and Narrator, Paul Scofield; Ebenezer Scrooge, Sir Ralph Richardson; Fred, Frederick Treves; First Gentleman & Spirit of Christmas Past, David Dodimead; Second Gentleman, Willoughby Goddard; Third Gentleman & Fezziwig, Norman Mitchell; Marley, Douglas Wilmer; Belle & Martha, Colette Wilde; Belle's Husband, Edgar Wreford; Spirit of Christmas Present, Willoughby Goddard; Bob Cratchet, James Culliford; Mrs. Cratchet, Pauline Jameson; Young Cratchet & Boy, John Mitchell; Tiny Tim, Michael Lewis.

1960 – **HARMONY RECORDS**. LP Reissue of Rathbone's 1942 78 rpms, with added Opening and Closing music by the Lynn Murray Singers.

12-24-1960 – WVNJ, Newark, N.J. 9-10pm. A Ronald Colman *Carol*, likely the 1941. Also, carols by the Rutgers Glee Club.

12-25-1960 – WBAI, New York. 10:15-10:45am. The 1951 Alec Guinness *Carol*.

12-25-1960 – WABC. 8-8:30pm. The Lionel Barrymore record.

12-17-1961 – NBC. (30m.) THE SINGING LADY. *Cast:* Ireene Wicker, Deems Taylor.

12-24-1961 – WJMA, Orange, Va. (30 min.) *Cast:* Scrooge, Lionel Barrymore.
   (Station owner Arch Harrison ran the 1947 record version every Christmas Eve during his tenure, from this date until 1984.)

1963 – **GOLDEN / WONDERLAND RECORDS**, LP102. "Merry Christmas." Reader: James Kenney. *Mus.:* The Golden Orchestra. (A musicalized *Carol*, plus other Christmas songs.)

12-08-1963 – WNYC. (25 min.) *Cast:* Ireene Wicker, Mary Winocur.

12-24-1965, 12-25-1965 – WTOD-AM & FM, Toledo, Ohio. AM: 4-4:45pm, 24th; FM: 9:30-10:15am, 25th. *Spons.:* Sterling Milk. *Cast:* The WTOD Players.
– Toledo Blade 12-23-1965

12-24-1965 – KPFK, Los Angeles. 7:30 (68 min.) *Prd., Dir.:* Henry Miller, David Ossman. *Wr.:* Ronald K. Siskind. *Cast:* KPFK Radio Repertory (inc. Norman Belkin?, Jeanne Sorrell?)

12-25-1965 – NBC. 10:05pm. MONITOR
Host, Gene Rayburn. (The 1947 MGM record, edited to 22 min.)
– Wisconsin State Journal 12-25-1965

12-25-1965 – BBC. (60 min.) *Prd., Wr.:* Charles Lefeaux? *Mus.:* Christopher Whelen. *Cast:* Narr. & Scrooge, Ralph Richardson; Bob Cratchit, Frederick Treves; Mrs. Cratchit, Mary Wimbush; Jacob Marley, John Ruddock; Ghost of Christmas Present, Ralph Truman; Ghost of Christmas Past, Wilfrid Carter; Fred, Bruce Beebe; Tiny Tim, Sheila Grant; Eric Anderson, Jo Manning Wilson, Rosilind Shanks.

1960s (Late?) – **FRANKLIN NATIONAL BANK**, LP HG-100. *Prd.:* Herb Gale. *Cast:* Peter Fernandez, Bill Griffis, Corinne Orr, The Regency Players; Narr., Ray Heatherton. (Based on Dickens' reading cut.)

1970's? – **WONDERLAND RECORDS**, 00339. 45 rpm. MR. MAGOO'S CHRISTMAS CAROL. W/ Readalong booklet. Music. Cast: Magoo/Scrooge, Jim Backus; Narr., Tom Cipolla.

1970s? – **POLYDOR RECORDS**. "Charles Dickens' 'A Christmas Carol' and other Yuletide Favorites - Featuring the voices of Carl Banas." (Music?) Inc: Is there a Santa Claus?/'Twas the Night Before Christmas/The Lord's Prayer.

12-24-1970 – WNBC, New York. (29 min.) *Cast:* Long John Nebel, Marv Albert, Ted Brown, Charles McCord, Jim Lowe.

1970 – BBC (Radio 4). STORY TIME. *Cast:* Scrooge, Patrick Magee.

12-??-1971 (?) – John Carradine performing linking narration of the songs from Basil Rathbone's 1956 TV musical, THE STINGIEST MAN IN TOWN.
    (See note in main body of book for this era.)

1972 – **CMS RECORDS**, CMS 634. LP. PORTRAITS FROM DICKENS
Cast: Scrooge, Patrick Magee; Anthony Jacobs, John Hollis, Cura, more. Side 1 – The *Carol*; Side 2 – Great Expectations. (From 1970 BBC broadcast above.)

1972 – **PETER PAN RECORDS**, LP 8110. The *Carol*, plus The Little Match Girl, and The Fir Tree. Peter Pan Players and Chorus.
    (*The same Carol seems to have seen rerelease as a 45 rpm Single and Cassette w/Readalong Book set.*)

1972 – **JABBERWOCKY RECORDS**; SOUNDELUX cassette;

later MIND'S EYE CLASSIC CD?; Broadcast? (50 min.) *Dir., Wr.:* Robert Lewis. *Cast:* Scrooge, Rick Cimino; Pat Franklyn, Bernard Mayes, Darryl Ferreira.

1973 – **LISTENING LIBRARY**, A 3386. LP/Cassette. (172 min.) *Reader:* Patrick Horgan. (Uncut text.)

1974 – **STERLING PRODUCTIONS**. 2 LPs. *Solo Perfomance, Wr.?:* Dr. Lestor L. Hale. *Mus:* Norwood Singers of Jacksonville; Baritone Steve Saxon of Gainesville.
   (Apparently recorded in two sessions, at the University in Gainesville and in Jacksonville.)

12-??-1974? – Possible broadcast of a Barrymore *Carol*, with added songs from the 1970 film. (See note in body of book for this era.)

1975 – **BBC RECORDS**, 186. SPOKEN WORD DICKENS. (Same content as 1972 CMS record above.)
"These are dramatisations of characters from the Radio 4 series 'Story Time', broadcast in 1970. The record gives us Patrick Magee as Scrooge in A Christmas Carol and John Hollis as Magwitch in Great Expectations. The first is extremely well done and gives us the essence of the story. The effects are effective and suitably spine-chilling, even if the echo-chamber, as so often, puts a strain on the ear. The story of Magwitch is, of course, only a part of Great Expectations, and this to me is not as successful as an entity. The supporting casts and narration are admirable, and the record should please a young public."
– Roger Wimbush, Gramaphone magazine 4-1975

1975 – **DISNEYLAND RECORDS**, #3811. With illustrated story booklet. (35 min.) *Prd.:* Buddy Baker, Alan Young. *Wr.:* Alan Young (and Alan Dinehart). *Mus. by, Cond. by:* Buddy Baker; *Lyrics:* Tom Adair, Francis Adair. *Cast:* The Disneyland Players: Scrooge, Scrooge McDuck (Alan Young); Bob Cratchit, Mickey Mouse (Alan Young, who sources say played Mickey just this one time in place of his normal voicer of that period, Jimmy

McDonald); Nephew, Donald Duck (Clarence Nash); Marley's Ghost, Goofy; Christmas Past, Merlin (Alan Young); Isobel, Daisy Duck; Christmas Present, Willie the Giant (Alan Dinehart); Mrs. Cratchit, Minnie Mouse; Tiny Tim, Morty Mouse (Alan Young?); Cratchit Kids, Ferdy Mouse and others; Christmas Future, The Witch from Snow White (unspecified characters played by Janet Waldo, Walker Edmiston.)

12-??-1975 – WHBI, Newark. (29m.)

12-24-75 – CBS. (60m.) CBS RADIO MYSTERY THEATER *Prd., Dir.:* Himan Brown. *Wr.,* Ian Martin. *Cast:* Scrooge, E.G. Marshall; Marian Seldes, Ian Martin, Evie Juster, William Redfield, Robert Dryden.
 (Annually rebroadcast through 1981)

1977 – **ARGO RECORDS**, ZSW584-5. Roy Dotrice as Charles Dickens. (Dicken's reading version.)

12-17-1978 – WMMG, Brandenburg, KY & Kentucky Network, Inc. (60 min.) Live from Diners Playhouse, Lexington.

1979 – **PAPERBACK AUDIO**. Cassette. (90 min.) *Reader:* Peter Bartlett.

12-??-1979 – KGO, San Francisco. (30 min.) *Prd.:* Bill Crone. *Dir., Wr.:* Jack Brooks & Ellen Brooks. *Sfx:* Crone, Ron Hargrave, Tony Wong, Bruce Schirmer. *Cast:* (Station staff) Scrooge, "Mayor" Art Finley; Ghost of Christmas Present, Jay Schneider; Ghost of Christmas Past, Kip Lynch; Ghost of Christmas Future & Closing Announcer, Bob Kinsman; Marley's Ghost, Al "Jazzbeaux" Collins; Bob Cratchit, Jim Altoff; Mrs. Cratchit, Elizabeth Ripp; Scrooge's nephew, Owen Spann; Scrooge's niece & Boy on Street, Susan Bannacek; The Fezziwigs, Jim Eason & Mary Ellen Clinton; Charity Solicitor, Ray Taliaferro; Charity Solicitor & Businessman, Tom Hunter; Businessmen, Joe Starky & Ed Baxter; Young Scrooge, Ronn Owens; Amy, Pam Cleland; Tiny Tim, Mary Ellen Clinton; Martha Cratchit, Arlene Trot;

Topper, Bob Trevor; Carolers: Trot, Lynch, Eason, Bannacek, Collins, Denise Peach.

1980 – WONDERLAND (GOLDEN/A.A.) RECORDS, WLP-331. Stereo. Cast:
The Wonderland Players. (Children's).

12-24-1980 – BBC. 8-9pm. *Musical. Prd., Wr.:* Bobby Jaye. *Mus.:* Ewen Williams; *Orch., Arr.:* David Francis; Nigel Brooks Singers. *Cast:* Scrooge & Charles Dickens, Roy Dotrice; Bob Cratchit, Ronald Hurdman; Fred, Michael McClain; Charitable Gentleman, Edward Kelsey; Marley, Preston Lockwood; Spirit of Christmas Past, James Thomason; Fezziwig, Timothy Bateson; Dick, John Bull; Scrooge as a boy & the lad, Judy Bennett; Scrooge as a young man, Steven Pacey; Fan & Mrs. Fezziwig, Marise Hepworth; Belle, Rosemary Barclay; Spirit of Christmas Present, William Fox; Mrs. Cratchit, Diana Olson; Peter, Russell Lewis; Tiny Tim, Simon Henderson; Old Joe, Benny Lee; Mrs. Dilber, Patricia Hayes.

12-25-1980 – WNEW-FM, New York. 12pm-12:30pm. *Prd., Dir.:* Richard Neer, Vin Scelsa. *Sfx:* Larry Fast. *Cast:* Scrooge, Scott Muni; Fred, Andy Fisher; Solicitor, Dennis Elsas; Bob Cratchit, Pete Fornatale; Marley's Ghost, Dave Herman; Ghost of Christmas Past, Tom Morrera; Ghost of Christmas Present, Vin Scelsa; Ghost of Christmas Yet To Come, Richard Neer; Mrs. Cratchit, Robin Sagan; Pam Merly, Street Boy; Bernie Bernard, Belle; Scrooge's Friends, Pete Larkin, Jim Monahan; Tiny Tim, B.J. Austin; Announcer, Dan Neer. *Engineers:* Mitch Katz (?), Charlie Conrad, Gary Rosen.
(The script is from the 1941/1949 Colman production.)

1980 – CAEDMON RECORDS. *Reader:* Tom Conti. (Abridged Text).

12-??-1981 – WOWO, Ft. Wayne, In. (30 min.) *Prd., Dr.:* Tim Goeglein & Jim Skimos. *Wr.:* Walter Hackett. *Cast:* Scrooge, Ron Gregory; Narrator, Jack Underwood; Bob Cratchit, Dave Russell;

Mrs. Cratchit, Lois Dinkel; First Ghost, Chris Roberts; Second Ghost, Bob Sievers; Third Ghost, Diana Updike; Ghost of Jacob Marley, Victor Locke; Fred, Jim Skimos; Gentleman, Tim Goeglein; Fan, Pam Dennis; Martha, Linda Losch; The Man, Mike Dyes; The Woman, Sally Francis; Boy at the end, Kevin Friel; Tiny Tim, Ron Buskirk; Host, Jerry Hoffmann.

12-??-1981 – WMCA, New York. 4pm-6pm? *Cast:* Scrooge, Bob Grant; Bob Cratchit, Ralph Howard; The Ghost of Christmas Past, Dan Meenan; The Ghost of Christmas Present, Mark Simone; Scrooge's Nephew Fred, Mike Thompson; The Ghost of Marley, Barry Gray; Candy Jones.

12-??-1983 – AMERICAN PUBLIC RADIO (Synd.) (100m.)

1987 – **BANTAM AUDIO**, BAP 087. (60min.) *Reader:* John Gielgud.

12-20-1988 – WLUP-AM, Chicago. *Wr.:* Tom Cramer (Goodman Theater script.) *Sfx:* Wes Harrison. *Cast:* Scrooge, Steve Dahl; Narrator & Bob Cratchit, Garry Meier; Young Scrooge, Bob Sirott; Jacob Marley, Paul Hogan; Fred, Bruce Wolf; Ghost of Christmas Past, Roger Ebert; Peter Cratchit, Mike Tomczak; Young Man, Michael Maggio: Wilhemina, Michael Sneed (then Sirott); Charity Collector Fish, Tom Thayer, Charity Collector Friar, Paul Blair; Gary Fencik, Diann Burns, Mary Ann Childers.
    (Broadcast from before a live audience at the Museum of Broadcast Communications, benefiting Big Brothers/Big Sisters of Metropolitan Chicago.)
– "God Save Us, Every One! Dahl Makes Mincemeat Of A Classic" – Steve Johnson, Chicago Tribune 12-23-1988

1990 – **DOVE AUDIO.** Cassette. (180 min.) *Reader:* Paul Scofield.

12-??-1990 – BBC. (90 min.) *Prd., Dir.:* Janet Whitaker. *Mus.:* Elizabeth Parker. *Cast:* Scrooge, Michael Gough; Narrator, Freddie Jones; Nephew, Douglas Hodge; Fezziwig, Timothy Bateson;

Robert Edison, Elizabeth Lindsay, Peter Woodthorpe, Anna Wing, Ronald Herdman, Douglas Hodge, Petra Markham, Danny Schiller, Vivian Pickles, Hugo Mendez, Maxine Audley, Joanna Myers, Andrew Wyncote, Terence Edmund, Emma Gregory, Ian Lindsay, Timothy Carlton, Danielle Allen, Henry Power, Louise Cannes, James Holland, Miriam Arten, Marlene Gordon, Simon Dowe.

1990 – NPR. *Cast:* Jonathan Winters, Mimi Kennedy.
(From Dickens' public reading edition).

1991 – **SIMON & SCHUSTER AUDIO**, 76932-4. Cassette, LP, CD? (Released November 1) *Cast:* Patrick Stewart.
(One-Man performance based upon Stewart's British & Broadway stage presentation of his own adaptation of Dickens' text.)

1995 – **PENGUIN AUDIOBOOKS**, PEN 179. Cassette, CD. *Reader:* GEOFFREY PALMER.
(Unabridged.)

1995 – **AUDIO PARTNERS**, 21115. 2 Cassettes. *Solo Performance:* Miriam Margolyes. (Unabridged.)

12-24-95 & 12-25-95 – WBAI. QUICKSILVER RADIO THEATER (On THE GOLDEN AGE OF RADIO and ARTS IN THE EVENING)
Prd., Wr.: Craig Wichman. *Dir.:* Jay Stern. *Mus.:* Mark Hollmann. *Sfx:* Clyde Baldo & the cast. *Engineer:* David Nolan. *Cast:* Scrooge, Craig Wichman; Narr. & Charity Gent, Anthony Cinelli; Bob Cratchit & Man in Street, John Prave; Mrs. Cratchit & Mrs. Dilber, Ghislaine Nichols; Ghost of Christmas Past, Deborah Barta; Fred & Belle's Husband, Joseph Franchini; Belle & Martha, Jodi Botelho; Tiny Tim & Turkey Boy, Elizabeth Stull; Marley & Ghost of Christmas Present, Tony Scheinman.

1996 – **GREATHALL PRODUCTIONS**, 1124-016. CD. (60 min.) A CHRISTMAS CAROL AND OTHER FAVORITES.

Storyteller: Jim Weiss. (With "The Gift of the Magi" and "Dick Spindler's Family Christmas.")

1996 – Syndicated. FOCUS ON THE FAMILY RADIO THEATRE *Prd.:* Dave Arnold. *Wr.:* Paul McCusker. *Cast:* Host, David Suchet; Narrator, Timothy Bateson; Scrooge, Tenniel Evans; Young Marley & Ghost of Christmas Yet to Come, Robert Benfield; Peter Cratchit & Errand Boy, Richard Brightiff; Second Charity Worker & Second Businessman, Justin Butcher; Frannie & Martha Cratchit, Jane Gambler; Cratchit Daughter & Servant Girl, Katy Glassborow; Bob Cratchit & Vicar, Peter Goodwright; Young Ebenezer & Undertaker, Michael Haughey; Bell &, Jane, Katherine Kellgren; Ghost of Christmas Past & Mrs. Cratchit, Polly March; Young Cratchit Son, Tom Mount; Mrs. Beadnell & Mrs. Dilber, Myra Sands; Nephew Fred, Philip Sherlock; First Businessman & Mr. Fezziwig, Mervyn Stutter; First Charity Worker & Jacob Marley, Joe Richard Syms; Tiny Tim & Boy Ebenezer, Matthew White.

(The production credits as source Noel Langley's screenplay for the 1951 film as well as Dickens' book. Recorded at The Soundhouse Ltd., London.).

1999 – **REDFIELD ARTS**. CD. *Mus.:* Bill Dickson. *Cast:* Mark Redfield.

(One-Man performance based upon Dickens' public reading edition.)

1999 – **MONTEREY MEDIA**. 2 Cassettes. (112 min.) *Music. Cast:* The St. Charles Players.

"The St. Charles Players provide a rousing, involving adaptation of Dickens' classic story."
– Children's Bookwatch

12-24-1999 – (And following.) WBZ, Boston. *Cast:* "The WBZ Holiday Players" – Scrooge, Gary LaPierre; Fred, Carl Stevens; Christmas Past, Deb Lawlor; Marley, Gil Santos; Narr., etc., Michael Coleman.

1-2000 – Macduff Entertainment. Online mp3. (90 min.) Multi-voice; very full text; heavy electronic sfx and mus.

2002 – WOUB (Ohio University) Center for Public Media/ WIRED FOR BOOKS online. *Prd:* David Kurz. Dir.: Karen M. Chan. *Sound Design/Harpist:* Yoko Mori. *Audio Engineer:* Randy Norris. *Audio Assistant:* Matthew Gabel. *Artist:* Kit DeBerry. *Cast:* Scrooge & Choir, Joe Balding; Amanda Bosley, Scrooge's Sister; First Businessman, Marvin Bowman; Peter Cratchit & Soloist, Christian Chan; Ghost of Christmas Present & Soloist & Choir, Christopher Coleman; Mrs. Cratchit, Christina Dalesandry; The Charwoman, Patricia Elisar; Third Businessman, Bryan Gibson; Marley's Ghost & Old Joe, Steve Haskins; Fred & Soloist & Choir, Kevin S. Kunz; Belle's Husband, David Kurz; Cratchit Child, Rachel Luce; Bob Cratchit, Ron Luce; Mrs. Fezziwig, Nicki Mazzocca; Party Guest & Choir, Christine Neumann; Niece & Choir, Leslie Palumbo; Fiddler, Nikos Pappas; The Laundress & Mrs. Dilber, Laura Parrotti; Cratchit Child, Rebekah Roediger; Tiny Tim, Thaddaeus Roediger; Niece & Sister & Choir, Tawna Rogers; Belle, Christina Salerno; Fourth Businessman, Tim Sharp; Ghost of Christmas Past, Kerry Sill; Turkey Boy, Nick Sill; Fezziwig, Terrence J. Smith; Martha, Jessica Street; Plump Sister & Choir, Linda Watkins; Second Businessman, David Whealey; Narr., Karen M. Chan.

   (*Audio presentation of UNABRIDGED TEXT, but for the trimming of some "he/she saids." More than a simple group reading, with music and effects; but not quite a fully adapted and shaped dramatization.*)

2003 – **LISTENING LIBRARY CD.** *Solo Performance:* Jim Dale. Music. (Complete Text).

12-12-2003 – WYRS, Manahawkin, N.J. 7-8pm (approx.). QUICKSILVER RADIO THEATER
Prd., Dir., Wr.: Craig Wichman. *Mus.:* Kyler Brown. *Sfx.:* Eevin Hartshough and Bernadette Fiorella. Engineers: Bob Wick and John Cahill. *Cast:* Scrooge & Narr., Craig Wichman; Bob Cratchit & Jacob Marley, Dan Renkin; Nephew Fred & ensemble, Elmer Fawcett; Charity Gentleman, Carl Block; Ghosts of

Christmas Past & Present, Rick Mellerup; Boy Scrooge & Tiny Tim, Nick Feeney; Mr. Fezziwig & Ensemble, Paul Hart; Belle & ensemble, Eevin Hartsough; Mrs. Cratchit & Mrs. Dilber, Bernadette Fiorella; Martha & Debtor Wife, Ellie Hart; Fred's Wife & Ensemble, Linda Reddington; Second Gossiper & Debtor Husband, Bob Smith.

(A slightly different script than Quicksilver's 1995 production, presented by the Stafford Township Historical Society, and broadcast live before an audience at the historic Old Baptist Church in Manahawkin, N.J.)

2004 – Sirius/XM Radio, 2005 and following. (67 min.)
COLONIAL RADIO THEATRE
Prd., Dir.: Jerry Robbins. *Mus.:* Jeffrey Gage. *Cast:* Scrooge, J.T. Turner; Marley, Robbins; Joseph Zamparelli, Frederick Rice, Deniz Cordell, Lincoln Clark, Cynthia Pape, Kimberly McClure, Amy Strack, James Turner.

2004 – **NAXOS AUDIOBOOKS**. 3 CDs. (193 min.) *Solo Performance:* Anton Lesser.
(Uncut Text.)

2005 – **SCARLETT RAT ENTERTAINMENT.** Online MP3, CD. (34 min.?) *Cast:* Jim Greene, Maria Wechsler, Shannon O'Brien, Dana McCain, Andy Nyland, April Rejman, others?
(Several voices—the other Ghosts?—speak in unison with Marley and Past. Recorded live at the First Presbyterian Church in Skaneateles, New York on December 4, 2004.)

11-2007 – (Webcast.) SPOKEN WORD AMERICA (63 min.)
NIGHT KITCHEN RADIO THEATER
Dir., Wr.: Arthur Yorinks. Mus.: Edward Barnes. *Cast:* Scrooge, Peter Gerety; Ivy Austin, Greg Hildreth, Richard Muenz, Alice Playten, Steven Rattazzi, Nikki Hislop; members of the Frank Sinatra School of the Arts Concert Choir.

12-24-2010 – WWNC/WMXF, N.C. (90 min., inc. 60 min. *Carol*, 30 min. music.) (Live performance recorded 12-9-2010.)

Prd., Adapt. by: Don Connelly. *Dir.:* Steve Carlisle. *Mus. by, Cond. by:* Bruce H. Frazier, w/ orchestra, soloists, choir. *Cast:* Scrooge, S. Carlisle; Ernest Chappell, D. Connelly; Welles & Fezziwig, Terry Nienhuis; Dickens, D.V. Caitlyn; Bob Cratchit, Brendan Braaten; Fred & Joe & Robert, Bob McMahan; Man & Christmas Present, Joel Knisley; Marley & Tiny Tim, Dan Rohrig; Christmas Past, Arthur Anderson; Belle & Mrs. Cratchit & Charwoman, Leah Hampton; Martha, Jessi Lawson; Children, Josh Thompson; Christmas Yet To Come, Amanda Kouri; Choir Boy, Garrett Pace; Soloists, Mary Kay Bauer, Dan Cherry; Ora Nichols, Sound Effects Lady, Amanda Proffitt; Assistant Sound Effects by Aaron D'Innocenzi; Wind Machine by Greg Dills; Engineering by Tim Neese.

(Recreation of the 1938 Campbell's *Carol*, utilizing the original script and adapting the original music. With A. Anderson from the original cast, as well as a doubling that appears unique to this production: Marley & Tiny Tim!)

5-42011 (Cataloging date.) – (Online.) LIBRIVOX (3 hr. 1 min.) *Prd., Edit. by:* Elizabeth Klett. *Cast:* Ebenezer Scrooge, Andy Minter; Fred, mb; Bob Cratchit, David Richardson; Gentleman, Martin Langer; Jacob Marley, Algy Pug; Ghost of Christmas Past, Tricia G; Fan & Tiny Tim, rashada; Young Scrooge & Peter Cratchit, Paul Andrews; Schoolmaster & Man 2, Peter Bishop; Fezziwig, John Steigerwald; Belle, Availle; Belle's Husband & Man 3, Levi Throckmorton; Ghost of Christmas Present, Barry Eads; Mrs. Cratchit, Arielle Lipshaw; Martha Cratchit & Girl, Christin Chapelle; Belinda Cratchit & Caroline, Amy Gramour; Scrooge's Niece, Veronica Jenkins; Niece's Sister, Liberty Stump; Man 1, David Lawrence; Man 4, Chris Donnelly; Man 5, Darren V; Charwoman, Kara Shallenberg; Old Joe, Tom Crawford; Mrs. Dilber, Sandra G; Caroline's Husband, Shea McNamara; Boy, Saab; Narrator, Klett.

(UNABRIDGED TEXT, but no effects or music; a group reading, rather than a full dramatization.)

12-16-2011 (7-8pm); 12-23(11am); 12-24 (4-5pm); 12-25 (12pm) – WPPB, L.I. *Prd., Wr.:* Bonnie Grice. *Dir.:* Michael

Disher. *Sound:* Kyle Lynch. *Cast:* Scrooge, Dan Becker; Narrator & Marley & Fezziwig, Josh Gladstone; Bob Cratchit, Paul Bolger; Mrs. Cratchit, Barbara Jo Howard; Fred, Young Scrooge, Tristan Vaughan; Ghost of Christmas Past, Brooke Alexander; Belle & Martha, Rosemary Cline; Belle's Husband, Brendan O'Reilly; Fan, Meryn Anders; Ghost of Christmas Present, Terrance Fiore; Tiny Tim, Katie Kneeland; Rupert Stow, Julia Tyson.
(Script based on 1939 Campbell's *Carol*.)
– Sag Harbor (L.I.) Express 11-30-2011

12-24-2011 (8-9pm); 12-25-2011 (6-7pm.) – WQXR. *Dir.:* Elliott Forrest. *Wr.:* Arthur Yorinks. *Mus.:* John Forster. Sound: Fred Newman. *Cast (WQXR/WNYC hosts):* Narrator, John Schaefer; Scrooge, F. Murray Abraham; Bob Cratchit, Jeff Spurgeon; Child & Tiny Tim & boy, Jalen Robinson; Nephew & Peter Cratchit, Jad Abumrad; Gentleman & Businessman 1, Richard Hake; Marley & Businessman 2, David Garland; Mrs. Dilber & Fan & Belinda, Naomi Lewin; Christmas Past, Nimet Habachy; Young Scrooge & Undertaker, Elliott Forrest; Fezziwig & Old Joe, Brian Zumhagen; Belle & Martha & Nephew's Wife, Lorraine Mattox; Christmas Present, Robert Krulwich; Mrs. Cratchit & Miss Eliza, Celeste Headlee.
(Recorded live at The Greene Space, NYC.)

*****

ADDENDA: The following productions require further confirmation and/or information.

12-??-1932/38? – NBC. 5:30pm. (24m.) THE SINGING STORY LADY. *Prd., Wr., Solo Performer:* Ireene Wicker; Announcer, Bob Brown. With Hans Christian Anderson's "The Ugly Duckling." (A recording is in the collection of the Paley Center, date uncertain.)

UNITED TRANSCRIPTION SERVICE Syndication. (29 min.)

THESAURUS Syndication. (53 min.) #1664/1665; previously released as #598/599.

1950s? – Emlyn Williams as Charles Dickens reading the *Carol*? (Per William Nadel.)

1960s? – **RCA VICTOR RECORDS**, ERA-227. 45 rpm. *Reader?*: Lloyd Nolan. Carol excerpt, "God Bless Us Everyone, plus "Is There A Santa Claus?"

1960's? – **ADVENTURE RECORDS**. Adventure Stories In Sound #9

1960s? – **OMNIVOX RECORDS**, LP P 3128. *Adapt., Prd.:* Sydney Stevens? *Cast:* Frank Thorton, Anne Baker, Frank Ball? Made in France, English language. Cover art by Chadar.

1961? – Produced by Fiona Bentley?

12—1965/81? – WBAL (Baltimore.) (62m.) *Cast:* Scrooge, Jack Lacy. (Paley Collection, date uncertain.)

1970s? – WNYC (also Pacifica stations?) SPOKEN WORDS. Broadcast of Caedmon record?

1980's? – (Also Aired?) Friends of Old Time Radio convention. Newark, NJ. Live production by The Dave Warren Players. *Cast:* Carl Amari?; William Nadel?.

BIBLIOGRAPHY/ SOURCES

INSTITUTIONS:

New York Public Library, Performing Arts Library (inc. the Billy Rose Collection)

New York Public Library, Main Branch

G. Robert Vincent Voice Library at Michigan State University
Paley Center for Media (New York)

BOOKS:

Alpert, Hollis. *The Barrymores.* Dial Press, 1964.

Anderson, Arthur. *Let's Pretend and the Golden Age of Radio.* BearManor Media, 2004.

Anderson, Arthur. *An Actor's Odyssey – Orson Welles to Lucky the Leprehaun.* BearManor Media, 2010.

Barrymore, Lionel (with Cameron Shipp.) *We Barrymores.* Appleton-Century-Crofts, 1951.

Buxton, Frank and Owen, Bill. *The Big Broadcast.* The Viking Press, Inc., 1972.

Callow, Simon. *Orson Welles: The Road to Xanadu.* Penguin Books, 1995.

Carter, Sydney H. (Compiler). *A Catalogue of 'Sterling' Cylinder Records.* (Ernie Bayly, Editor.) 1975.

Davis, Paul. *The Life and Times of Ebenezer Scrooge.* Yale University Press, 1990.

DeLong, Thomas A. *Radio Stars – An Illustrated Biographical Dictionary of 953 Performers, 1920 through 1960.* McFarland & Company, Inc., 1996.

Dickens, Charles. *A Christmas Carol. In Prose. Being a Ghost Story of Christmas.* Chapman & Hall, 1843.

--------------------. *A Christmas Carol. In Prose. Being a Ghost Story of Christmas.* (Introduction by Lionel Barrymore.) Garden City Publishing Co., Inc., 1938.

Dunning, John. *On the Air: The Encyclopedia of Old-Time Radio.* Oxford University Press, 1998.

Guida, Fred and Wagenknecht, Edward. *A Christmas Carol And Its Adaptations: A Critical Examination of Dickens's Story And Its Productions on Screen And Television.* McFarland, 2006.

Hearn, Micheal Patrick. *The Annotated Christmas Carol.* W.W. Norton & Company, Inc. 2004.

Kobler, John. *Damned in Paradise.* Atheneum, 1977.

Kotsilibas-Davis, James. *The Barrymores.* Crown Publishers, Inc., 1981.

Peters, Margot. *The House of Barrymore.* Alfred A. Knopf, 1990.

Rathbone, Basil. *In and Out of Character.* Doubleday, 1962.

Sammon, Paul. *The Christmas Carol Trivia Book.* Citadel Press, 1994.

Welles, Orson and Bogdanovich, Peter (Jonathan Rosenbaum, Editor). *This Is Orson Welles.* Da Capo Press, 1998

PERIODICALS (SPECIFIC DATES CITED WITHIN TEXT:)

Variety
Life
The Saturday Evening Post
Misc. Newspapers

OTHER PUBLICATIONS:

Hickerson, Jay. *The New, Revised Ultimate History of Network Radio Programming and Guide to All Circulating Shows.* Presto Print II, 1996.
Misc. OTR catalogs.

ONLINE RESOURCES:

Archive.org.
Digital Deli, The.
Ernie (Not Bert).
Gramophone.
Internet Broadway Database, The.
Music Discographies at bjbear71.com, The.
The Old Time Radio Digest.
Old Time Radio Researchers Group, The (esp. inc. JJ's Newspaper Radio Logs).
Olde Tyme Radio Network, The.
Quiet, Please Forum.
Radio GOLDINdex.
Tinfoil.com (Glenn Sage)
Yule Log.com (Lawrence F. "Chip" Arcuri)

CONVERSATIONS/INTERVIEWS/CORRESPONDENCE WITH:

AN ANONYMOUS BENEFACTOR.

ARTHUR ANDERSON.

JULIE ASHTON.

Michael Biel.

Jane Blalock.

Lonnie Burr.

Don Connelly.

Tommy Cook.

Bob Grant.

Fred Guida.

Michael C. Gwynne.

Jimmy Lydon.

Shirley Mitchell.

William Nadel.

Bill Owen.

Dick Van Patten.

Margot Peters.

Simon "Stuffy" Singer.

Bob Statzer.

Jay Stern.

INDEX

PLEASE NOTE —
This index covers the main body of the book Staves 1-7 and the appended Log. Names of publications and titles of fictional and dramatic works are *italicized*; the latter are radio productions except when further described in parentheses as (book, play, movie, etc.) A listing in "quotation marks" is a character name. Wherever possible, cast and crew information is reproduced exactly as found in the original productions' documentation. Page numbers in *italics* denote illustrations and captions.

8mm (film format) 149
A.A. Records (see also Golden, Wonderland) 192
A.O. Smith (co.) *71*, 181, 182
Abbott, Diane 182
Abraham, F. Murray 159, 199
Abumrad, Jad 199
Adair, Francis 190
Adair, Tom 190
Adler, Stella 149
Adventure Records (Adventure Stories In Sound) 200
Adventures of Paul and Marian, The (movie) 150
Adventures of Superman (TV series) 131
Adventures of Tom Sawyer (1938 movie) 41, 50
Albert, Marv 145, 189
Alexander, Brooke 199
Alexander, Francis *9*
All in the Family (TV series) 142
Alland, William *48*
Allen, Arthur 25, 170, 171
Allen, Danielle 194
Allendale, NJ 29
Algonquin Round Table 29
Alpert, Hollis 63
Altoff, Jim 191
Amari, Carl 200
American Broadcasting Company (ABC) 57, 58, 67, 88, 146, 179
American Public Radio 140, 193
American Radio Theatre 87
Amos 'n' Andy 19
Amsbury, Wallace Bruce 164

Anders, Meryn 159
Anderson, Alice 156
Anderson, Arthur 25, 43–(*45, 48*)-54, 64, 95, 97, 116, 156 -*158*, 174, 198
Anderson, Eddie "Rochester" 180
Anderson, Eric 188
Andrews Sisters *67*, 180
Andrews, Paul 198
Apollo Club Chorus 32, 173
Archer, Claude 170
Argo/Spoken Arts Records 126, 186, 191
Armed Forces Radio Service (AFRS) 58-59, 178, 180
Arnold, Dave 195
Arnold, Edward 76, 184
Arten, Miriam 194
Arts In The Evening (WBAI) 194
As Time Goes By (TV series) 129
Ashton, Julie 93-95, 97
Associated Press (AP) 66, 179, 186,
Atwood, Genevieve 184
Audio Book Co. 127, *127*, 186
Audio Partners 194
Audley, Maxine 194
Austin, B.J. 192
Austin, Ivy 197
Autry, Gene *67*, 180
Availle 198
Bach Choir 187
Bacher, William A. 177
Backus, Georgia
Backus, Jim 15, 123, *123*, 189
Baer, Parley 74, 76, 86, 183
Baker, Anne 200
Baker, Buddy 190
Balding, Joe 196

Baldo, Clyde 154, 194
Ball, Frank 200
Ballinger, Art 182, 183
Banas, Carl 133, 189
Bannacek, Susan 191
Bantam Audio 193
Barbour, E. Livingston 170
Barclay, Rosemary 192
Barks, Carl 194
Barlow, Howard 23, 170, 171, 172
Barnes, Edward 197
Barnes, Tommy 177
Barnett, Sonny 181, 182
Barnum (Broadway musical) 129
Barrier, Edgar 49, 174, 175
Barror, Cecil 186
Barrymore, Drew 32
Barrymore, Ethel 32, 37, 80, 99
Barrymore, John 32, 37, 38-*40*, 173, 183
Barrymore, John Jr. 115
Barrymore, Lionel (Lionel Herbert Blythe) *Frontpiece*, 31-(*31, 33, 35, 40, 45, 48, 52, 56, 58, 60, 66, 67, 71, 72, 77-80*)-80, 91, 103, 111-(*112, 114*)-116, 119, 135, 137, 142, 145, 155, 173-188, *Back Cover*
Barrymores, The (Alpert book) 63
Barrymores, We (book) 38
Barta, Deborah 154, 194
Bartlett, Peter 130, 191
Bateson, Timothy 138, 140, 192, 193, 195
Battis, William Sterling 95, 121, 162
Bauer, Mary Kay 198
Baxter, Ed 191

Beals, Dick (Richard) 76, 183
Beals, John 181
Beaty, Mary Rodgers *120*, 185
Beauty and the Beast (TV series) 129
Beck, Jackson 53, 147
Becker, Dan 199
Beebe, Bruce 188
Belkin, Norman 142, 188
Bell, Don 170
Bell, Shirley 19
Benaderet, Bea 175
Benfield, Robert 195
Bennett, Judy 192
Benny, Jack *67*, 73, 87
Bentley, Fiona 200
Berens, Harold 187
Berg, Charles F. 18
Bernard, Bernie 192
Best Actor of 1942-1943 (radio poll) 57, 178
Bible, The 43, 118, 119, 167
Big Broadcast, The (book) 78
Big Brothers/Big Sisters of Metropolitan Chicago 193
Billboard (publication) 182, 187
Birkenholz, Arcadie 18, 168
Bishop, Peter 198
Blair, Henry 181
Blair, Paul 193
Blalock, Jane 105
Block, (Mayor) Carl 155, 196
Bloomington, Indiana 156, *157*
Blue Network (NBC) 18
Blunt, Gabriel 182
Boar's Head Dramatic Society 18, 166
Bob Brown 199
Bogarde, Dirk 88, 180

Bolger, Paul 199
Bond, Derek 180
Booth, W.R. 12
Bosley, Amanda 196
Boston Globe 163, 164, 166-168
Botelho, Jodi 154, 194
Bourbon, Diana 54
Bowman, Marvin 196
Braaten, Brendan 198
Bradley, Truman 174
Braine, Ruth 164
Briar, Denise 182
Brice, Fanny 63, 174
Bridgeport (CT) *Telegram* 162, 164, 168
Brightiff, Richard 195
British Broadcasting Corporation (BBC) 13, 26, 129, 88, 129, 131, 132, 138, 173, 177, 182, 186, 188-190, 192, 193
Broekman, David 177
Brooks, Ellen 191
Brooks, Jack 191
Brown, Helen 176
Brown, Himan 139, 191
Brown, Kyler 196
Brown, Ted 189
Bryan, Arthur Q. 79, *84*, 85, 105, 177, 181
Bull, John 192
Bull, Peter 184
Burgum, Mary 16, 162
Burnett, Harry LeRoy 182
Burns (George) and Allen (Gracie) *67*, 180
Burns, Diann 193
Burpee, Vora 167
Burr, Lonnie 85-87, 119, 183

Burrell, John 177
Bushman, Francis X. 105, 108, 177
Buskirk, Ron 193
Butcher, Justin 195
Butterfield, Herb 74, 183
"C.C." (reviewer) 105
Caedmon Records 138, 187, 192
Cahill, John 196
Caitlyn, D.V. 198
Camden (RCA) Records 184
Campbell Playhouse 41, *45*, 51, *96, 157, 158*, 174, 175
Campbell Soup Company 34, 41-43, 49, 51, 54, 55, *96*, 111, *157*, 173-175, 198, 199
Cannes, Louise 194
Canterbury Choir 179
Capehart (Radio/TV manufacturer) 65, *66*
Capeheart Christmas Hour 66, 68
Capra, Frank 32, 76
Carlin, Steven R. 118, 182
Carlisle, Steve 198
Carlson, J. Ralph 99, *102*, 176
Carlson, Richard 99, *102*
Carlton, Henry Fiske 25
Carlton, Timothy 194
Carmichael, Coralie 186
Caroleers, The 187
Carradine, John 140, 189
Carter, Wilfrid 138, 188
CBS Columbia Square (radio studio) 74, *75*
CBS Radio Mystery Theater 139, 191
Centralia (WA) Daily Chronicle 169
Chadar 200
Chan, Christian 196
Chan, Karen M. 135, 196

Chandler, Gloria 162
Chapelle, Christin 198
Chapman, Donald 176
Chappell, Ernest 18, 53, 79, 90, *93-96*, 97-99, 103, 126, 147, 150, 166, 174-176, 179, 184, 198
Charleston (WV) Daily Mail 51
Charlesworth, John 182
Chatterton, Larry 182
Chekov, Anton 138
Cherry, Dan 198
Chicago Tribune 144, 162-178, 193
Childcraft Records (see also Mercury) 121, 187
Childers, Mary Ann 193
Christ Lutheran Church, NYC 149
Christian Science Monitor 169
Christmas At The Front 178
Christmas Carol, A (1938 movie) 42, 55, 88
Christmas Carol, A (1947 TV broadcast) 140
Christmas Carol, A (1984 TV movie) 59, 139
Christmas Carol, A (1999 TV movie) 133
Christmas Carol, A (book) 9-(*11*)-12, 25, 28, 34, 61, 68, 75, 78, 97, 108, 127, 150, 159, 161, 186, 190, 194
Christmas Carol—In Eight Minutes, A (movie) 155
Christmas Festival 180
Christmas Party 58, 173
Christmas Tree, The (record story) 187
Christmas with the Stars 103
Church, Rev. E. F. 163

Church, Wilda Wilson 166
Cimino, Rick 190
Cinderella (musical) 99
Cinelli, Anthony 154, 194
Cipolla, Tom 123, 189
CKLW Detroit 90, 184
CKY Winnipeg 163
Clarence (radio play) 43
Clark, Don 23, 170-172, 179, 183
Clark, Lincoln 197
Clark, Lon 65
Classical Recordings (publication) 105
Clay, Nicholas 187
Clay, Nigel 187
Clay, Rachel 187
Cleland, Pam 191
Cleveland Plain Dealer 163, 165, 167, 170, 171
Cline, Rosemary 199
Clinton, Mary Ellen 191
CMS Records 189, 190
Coggeshall, Asa O. 163
Colchester Ensemble 166
Cold War 69
Coleman, Christopher 196
Coleman, Michael 195
College of Wooster 171
Collins, Al "Jazzbeaux" 142, 191, 192
Collins, Ray 47, 53, 174, 175
Collyer, Clayton "Bud" (Collier, Bud) 98, 99, 176
Colman, Ronald 83-(*84*)-85, 103, *104*, 117, 119, 121, 124, 126, 137, 147, 175, 181, 184-187, 192
Colonial Radio Theatre 156, 197
Colorado Springs 94
Colton, Kingsley 47, 174

Columbia Broadcasting System (CBS) *Frontpiece*, 11, *21, 27, 31, 33, 35, 45, 52, 56, 72, 75, 82, 157, 158*, 170-175, 178-185
Columbia Records 80, 104, 118, 177
Connell, Denis E. 184
Connelly, Don 156, *157*, 198
Conover, Jean 170
Conrad, Charlie 192
Conried, Hans 103, *104*, 174, 177, 178, 182
Conti, Tom 130, 192
Cook, Tommy 55, 84, 103, 105-(*107*)-110, 177
Copeland, Prof. Charles Townsend 168
Copperhead, The (stage play) *77*
Cordell, Deniz 197
Corwin, Norman 110
Coshocton (OH) Tribune 164
Cotten, Joseph 46, 176
Cottrell, William D. 182
Coulouris, George 53, 175
Cramer, Tom 193
Crawford, Joan 51
Crawford, Tom 198
Crenna, Richard 74
Cricket Records 119, 183
Croft, Mary Jane 74
Crone, Bill 191
Crosby, Bing *67*, 103
Crowder, Leslie 182
Culliford, James 187
Cura 189
D'Innocenzi, Aaron 198
Dahl, Steve 144, 193
Dale, Jim *128*, 129, 196
Dalesandry, Christina 196

Damroth Players 172
"Dan Pegotty" *33, 77*
Daniell, Henry 179
Danny Kaye 180
Darby, Ken *104*,175
Dari-Rich *82*
Dasch, George 167
Date With Judy, A 109
Dave Warren Players 200
Davey and Goliath (TV series) 76
David Copperfield (1935 film) *33, 77*, 80
Davis, Dix 55, 79, 109, 177
De Corsia, Ted 183
DeBerry, Kit 196
Decatur (WA) Review 19, 170
Decca Records 85, 103, *104*, 175, 181
Defiance, OH 103, 159
Dennis the Menace (1959 TV series) 59
Dennis, Pam 193
Devine, Evelyn 176
Van Patten, Dick/Richard (Van Patton) 25, 98-99, 176
Dick Spindler's Family Christmas (record story) 195
Dickens, Charles 9-(*11*)-13, 16, 28-29, 32, 34, 36-38, 69, 85, 95, 97, 125-126, *130*, 133, 140, 145, 147, 149, 155-156, 159, 182, 189, 192
Dickson, Bill 195
Dills, Greg 198
Dinehart, Alan 124, 190, 191
Diners Playhouse (Lexington, Ky.) 142, 191
Dinkel, Lois 193

Disher, Michael 199
Disney Studio 74, 85, 124-125, 154, 190
Disneyland Records 124, *125*, 190
Dobkin, Lawrence 183
Dodimead, David 187
Don Cossack's Russian Male Chorus 32, 173
Don Juan in Hell (stage play) 118
Don Lee Hollywood Playhouse 176
Don Lee Network 176
"Donald Duck" 125, *125*, 191
Donaldson, Ted 79, *80*, 176
Donnelly, Chris 198
Donnolly, James 176
Dorn, George 184
Dotrice, Roy 129, *130*, 138, 140, 191, 192
Douglas, Paul 178
Douglass, Elmer 165, 167
Dove Audio 193
Dowe, Simon 194
Dowling, Vincent 186
Doyle, Brenda 186
Doyle, Sir Arthur Conan 26
Dr. Paul 86
Dracula (book) 126
Drama Desk Award 135
Dramatic Club of the Big Brother Hour 166
Drews, the (acting family) 32, 37
Dryden, Robert 139, 191
Duffy's Tavern 99
Dumont (TV network) 65
Dyce, Hamilton 182
Dyes, Mike 193
Eads, Barry 198
Eason, Jim 191, 192

'Eathen, The (radio poem) 168
Ebert, Roger 145, 193
Edison (movie) Studio 12
Edison Records (British) 13-*14*, 162
Edison, Robert 194
Edmiston, Walker 125, 191
Edmund, Terence 194
Eight is Enough (TV series) 99
Elisar, Patricia 196
Elliot, Larry 178
"Elmer Fudd" 84
Elsas, Dennis 192, 147
EMI Records 187
Entriken, Knowles 65
Episcopal Actors' Guild 156
Erickson, Louise 109
Erie Canal 44
Ernie [Not Bert] Blogspot *117*
ET (Electric Transcription) 100, 101
Evans, Harold 88, 182
Evans, Reynolds 170
Evans, Tenniel 195
Every Man's Theater 108
F. Murray Abraham 159, 199
Farber, Jerry 181
Farrington, George 184
Fast, Larry 192
"Father Christmas" 159
Favorite Story 83, 84, 85, 181
Fawcett, Elmer 196
Feeney, Nick 155, 197
Fencik, Gary 193
Fennelly, Parker 170
Fenwick, Irene 38
Fernandez, Peter 132, 189
Ferreira, Darryl 190
Fibber McGee and Molly 87

Field, Elizabeth 164
Finch, Matthew 154
Finley, "Mayor" Art 142, 191
Finn, Cleland 182
Finney, Albert 142
Fiore, Terrance 199
Fiorella, Bernadette 99, 155, 196, 197
Fir Tree, The (record story) 189
Firesign Theatre 142
First Presbyterian Church (Skaneateles, NY) 197
Fisher, Andy 192
Fiske, Henry 25, 171
Focus on the Family Radio Theatre 140
Forbes, Brenda 174
Fornatale, Pete 147, 192
Forrest, Elliott 199
Forster, John 199
Forsyth, Tom 175
Fort Rouge Methodist Church (Winnipeg) 163
Fox, William 192
Franchini, Joseph 154, 194
Francis, David 192
Francis, Derek 187
Francis, Sally 193
Frank Sinatra School of the Arts Concert Choir 197
Frankenstein (radio play) *153*
Franklin National Bank 133
Franklyn, Pat 190
Fraser, Ruth 184
Frazier, Bruce H. 198
Frehm, Ray 100
Freud, Sigmund 38
Friel, Kevin 193

Friends of Old Time Radio
  Convention (FOTR) 98, 106, 200
Frost, Alice 47, 174
Froug, William 183
G, Sandra 198
G, Tricia 198
Gabel, Matthew 196
Gage, Jeffrey 197
Gale (Galewitz), Herb 133, 189
Gambler, Jane 195
Garbett, Arthur S. 166
Garbo, Greta 34
Garden City Pub. Co. 60
Garland, David 199
Garson, Greer *107*
Gentile, Joe 184
George Olson Orchestra 173
"George Spelvin" 48-49, 174
Gerard, Marie 170
Gerety, Peter 197
Gerson, Betty Lou 182
Gibson, Bryan 196
Gibson, John 176
Gielgud, John 88, 121, 130, 132, 193
Gift of the Magi, The (record story) 195
Gillette, William 53
Gilmore, Iris Ruth 167
Gish, Lillian 83
Gladstone, Josh 199
Glassborow, Katy 195
Gleaner (Jamaica newspaper) 20, 21, 23, 170
Gleason, Jackie 146
Globe Theater 59, 178
Goblins who Stole a Sexton, The (prose story) 10

Goddard, Willoughby 187
Goeglein, Tim 145, 192, 193
Golden Age Of Radio, The (WBAI) 194
Golden Legends 169
Golden Records (see also A.A., Wonderland) 119-(*120*)-122, 185, 188, 192
Good News of 1939 (*Maxwell House presents*) 42, 174
Goodbye, Mr. Chips (radio play) *107*
Goodman Theatre 144
Goodwright, Peter 195
"Goofy" *125*, 191
Gordon, Gale 103, *104*,176
Gordon, Gavin 174, 181
Gordon, Marlene 194
Gordon, Richard 26, 98, 171, 176
Gospel of Luke 43
Goss, Frank 183
Gough, Michael 138-140, 193
Gould, Jay 145
Gramophone (magazine) 126, 132
Gramour, Amy 198
Grant, Bob 146, 147, 193
Grant, Sheila 188
Gray, Barry 146, 147, 193
Great Depression 67
Great Expectations (record story) 189, 190
Great Gildersleeve, The ("Why The Chimes Rang") 75, 109
Greathall Productions 194
Green, Martyn *141*
Greene Space, NYC 199
Greene, Jim 197
Gregg, Virginia 183
Gregory, Emma 194

Gregory, Ron 145, 192
Grice, Bonnie 199
Griffith, D.W. (David Wark) 32
Grimes, Jack 25
Groom, Stanley 182
"Gros." (reviewer) 69
Gross, Walter 180
Guideposts (magazine) 69, 180
Guinness, Alec 88, 132, 180, 187
Gwenn, Edmund 79-(*80*)-81, 83, 85, 176, 181-183
Gwynne, Michael C. 113-116
Habachy, Nimet 199
Hackett, Walter 145, 192
Hahn, Helen *17*
Hale, Dr. Lester L. 129-130, 190
Hale, Richard 112, 133, 179
Hall, Dickie *114*
Hall, Lansing 184
Hallmark Hall of Fame, The 70, 183, 184
Hallmark Playhouse 70, *72*, 182
Hallowe'en (Lionel Barrymore music) 116
Halloween 41, *153*
Hamilton (OH) Daily News 169
Hammer Studios 138
Hammond Organ 93, 100
Hampden, Burford 176
Hampton, Leah 198
Harding, Lucille A. 164
Harding, Michael 182
Hardwicke, Sir Cedric 137, 185
Harford, Alec 55
Harford, Betty 182
Hargrave, Ron 191
Harmony Records 187
Harris, Phil 73

Harrison, Arch 137, 188
Harrison, Wes 193
Harry Potter (movie series) 129
Hart, Ellie 197
Hart, Paul 197
Hartford (CT) Courant 26, 167, 169-172
Hartshough, Eevin 155, 197
Harvey, Trevor 182
Haskins, Steve 196
Haughey, Michael 195
Hawley, Mark 170
Hay, Bill 19, 165, 167, 168
Hayes, Patricia 192
"Head Elf" 133
Headlee, Celeste 199
Heartbeat Theatre 86, 87, 119
Heatherton, Ray 133, 189
Heminghous, Paula 176
Henderson, Simon 192
Henderson, Skitch 176
Henry Aldrich (movie series) 84
Hepworth, Marise 192
Hercule Poirot (TV series) 140
Herdman, Ronald 194
Herman, Dave 192
Herrmann, Bernard *48*, 49, 53, 57, 174, 175
Herz, Bill (William) 49, 174
Hicks, Barbara 187
Hildreth, Greg 197
Hislop, Nikki 197
Historyforsale.com 112
Hitchcock, Alfred 79
Hodge, Douglas 138, 193, 194
Hoffmann, Jerry 193
Hogan, Paul 193
Holland, James 194

Hollis, John 189, 190
Hollmann, Mark 154, 194
Holloway, Jean 57, 178, 179
Hollywood Hotel 34, 38, 41, 173
Hollywood Theater (Of Stars) 181
Hopper, Hedda *67*, 180
Horgan, Patrick 129, 190
House of Barrymore, The (book) 39
Howard, Barbara Jo 199
Howard, Ralph 193
Howdy Doody – A Christmas Carol (record) 119, *120*, 185
Howdy Doody (TV series) 119
Hughes, Donald (Don) 25-*27*, *170*, 171
Hugo Peretti Orchestra 187
Hull, Warren 174
Hunchback of Notre Dame, The (1939 movie) 118
Hunt, Althea 175
Hunter, Tom 191
Hurdman, Ronald 192
Huston, Noah 177
Imus, Don 145
In and Out of Character (book) 80, 178
Inner Sanctum Mysteries 86, 139
International Tennis Hall of Fame 110
Invisible Man, The (movie) 121
Iowa City Press-Citizen 164
Is There A Santa Claus? (record story) 189, 200
It's A Wonderful Life (movie) 32, 77
iTunes 155
J. Arthur Rank Organization 87, 180
Jabberwocky Records 189
Jack Benny Program, The 73, 87

Jacobs, Anthony 187, 189
Jacques Orchestra, The 187
Jameson, Pauline 187
Jasden (sp?), Larry 182
Jaye, Bobby 192
Jenkins, Veronica 198
Johns, Vere Everette 20-(*21*)-24, 170
Johnson, Lamont 183
Johnson, Steve 144, 193
Johnstone, Bill 181, 183
Jones, Candy 146-147, 193
Jones, Freddie 138, 193
Jonny Quest (TV series) 76
Joslyn, Allyn 24, 170
Journal-Times (Racine, WI) 66, 179
Juggler of Notre Dame, The (radio story) 180
Julius Caesar (stage play) 44
Jung, Carl 38
Juster, Evie 139, 191
Kane, Byron 69, 177, 181-183
Katz, Mitch 192
Kaye, Danny *67*
KDKA Pittsburgh 16, 164, 165, 167-169
Kearns, Joseph 59, 69, 76, 79, 84, 147, 174, 178, 181, 182, 183
"Keebler Elf" 76
Kellgren, Katherine 195
Kelly, Tommy 41, 173
Kelsey, Edward 192
Ken Dodd Show, The 186
Kendall, Cyrus (Cy) *104*, 176, 181
Kennedy, Mimi 140, 194
Kenny, James 121
Kentucky Network, Inc. 142, 191
Kester, Max 177
KFWB Los Angeles 172

KGO San Francisco/Oakland 16-18, 142-143, 166, 191
KGW Portland 18, 169
KHJ Los Angeles 173
King George VI 55
King, Dennis 65
Kingston (NY) Daily Freeman 171
KKFI Kansas City, MO 149
Klein, Arthur Luce 126, 186
Kleiner, Richard 116
Klett, Elizabeth 135, 198
Kneeland, Katie 199
Knight, Frank 170
Knisley, Joel 198
KOA Denver 167
Koch, Howard 52, 111, 174
Kokomo Tribune 167
Kouri, Amanda 198
Koury, Rex 182
KPFK Los Angeles 142, 188
Krasno, Hecky 118
Krulwich, Robert 199
Kruschen, Jack 86
Kunz, Kevin S. 196
Kurz, David 196
KYDL Salt Lake City 180
KYW Chicago 162, 165
Lacy, Jack 200
Langer, Martin 198
Langley, Noel 140, 195
LaPierre, Gary 145, 195
Larkin, Pete 192
Laughton, Charles 103, 117-119, 121, 182
Lawlor, Deb 195
Lawrence, David 198
Lawrence, Raymond 177, 182, 183
Lawson, Jessi 198

Lean, David 121
Lean, Dr. Delbert G. 171
LeCornec, Bill (Billy) 120, 185
Lee, Benny 192
Lee, Bill 124
Lee, Harriet 170
Leech, John 10-*11, 104*
Leeds, Earl 181
Lefeaux, Charles 138, 188
Lehman, Frieda (Freeda Lehmann) 164, 166
Leno, Charles 182
Lesser, Anton 130, 197
Let's Pretend 25, 47, 49, 98, 99
Lethbridge (Alberta) Herald 167
Levy, Ted 162
Lewin, Naomi 199
Lewis, Elliot 105, 108, 177
Lewis, Martin 182
Lewis, Michael 187
Lewis, Robert 190
Lewis, Russell 192
Library Journal 154
LibriVox 135, 198
Life (magazine) 59, *60, 114*
Life of Riley, The 109
Life With Father (radio play) 44
Light of the World 119
Lillie, Beatrice (Bea) 32, 173
Lilly Library *157*
Lindsay, Elizabeth 194
Lindsay, Ian 194
Lindsay, John 141
Lipshaw, Arielle 198
Listening In (newspaper column) 19, 170
Listening Library *128*, 196
Lithuanian (language) 90, 177

Little Church Around The Corner, The (NYC) 156
Little Match Girl, The (record story) 189
Little Orphan Annie 19
Little Symphony of Chicago 167
Littlest Angel, The (radio/record) 103
Locke, Victor 193
Lockhart, Gene 42, 174
Lockhart, June 177
Lockhart, Kathleen 42, 55, 174, 177
Lockwood, Margaret 87, 180
Lockwood, Preston 192
Loebell, Mark 170
Loekle, Harold F. 28-29, 51, 68, 89, 150, 172
Longines Symphonette 180
Lonnie Burr Collection, The 87
Lord's Prayer, The (record selection) 189
Los Angeles Times 172, 176
Losch, Linda 193
Losey, Frederick D. 163
Lost Horizon (1937 movie) 83
Lovell, Leigh 26, 171
Lowe, Jim 189
Lowell (MA) Sun 164, 168
Lowther, George 65
Luce, Rachel 196
Luce, Ron 196
"Lucky, the Lucky Charms Leprechaun" 43
Lucy Show, The (TV series) 103
Ludlam, George P. 26, 172
Lung, Charlie 182
Lydon, Jimmy 25, 84, 181
Lynch, Kip 191
Lynch, Kyle 199

Lynn Murray Singers 187
Macduff Entertainment 196
MacGregor, C.P. 41, 174, 181
Mack, Dick 181
Mack, Helen 109
Mack, Nila 25
Mackaye, Fred *104*, 176
MacWhorter, Rev. Gardner A. 162
Magee, Patrick 138, 189, 190
Maggio, Michael 193
Mama (aka *I Remember Mama*) (TV series) 99
Man Who Came To Dinner, The (stage play) 29
Manitoba Free Press 163
Manley, William Ford 25, 171
March, Fredric 57, 177
March, Hal *67*, 74, 180
March, Polly 195
Margolyes, Miriam 129, 194
Marin, Edwin L. 174
Markham, Petra 194
Markle, Fletcher 108
Marshall, E.G. 139-140, 191
Marshall, Herbert 59, 180
Martin Chuzzlewit (book) 10
Martin, Frank 58, 59, 178, 180
Martin, Ian 139, 191
Martin, Tony 174
Mattox, Lorraine 199
Maxwell, Ted 169
Mayer, Louis B. 66
Mayers, Frederick P. 167
Mayes, Bernard 190
Mayor of the Town 56-(58)-60, 65-67, *72*, 178-180
Mazzocca, Nicki 196
McCain, Dana 197

McCallum, John 180
McClain, Michael 192
McClure, Kimberly 197
McCord, Charles 145, 189
McCusker, Paul 140, 195
McDermott, Grace 16, 162
McDonald, Jimmy 125, 190
McDonnell, Craig 176
McGovern, John 176
McKenna, Siobhan 131, 186
McKnight, Tom (McNight) 104, 177
McMahan, Bob 198
McMaster, Anew 131, 186
McNamara, Shea 198
McNear, Howard 174, 181
Meenan, Dan 193
Meier, Garry 193
Meiser, Edith 26, 104-105, 171, 177
Mellerup, Rick 155, 197
Mendez, Hugo 194
Menken, Shepard 181, 182
Mercury Records (see also Childcraft) 121, 187
Mercury Theatre 41-(*45, 48, 52*)-57, 98, 121, 156, *157, 158*, 159, 174, 175, 198, 199
Merker, Mary 176
"Merlin" (Disney character) *125*, 191
Merly, Pam 192
Merrill, Lou 55, *104*, 175, 177
Messiah (G.F. Handel music) 15, 18
Metro-Goldwyn-Mayer (MGM) 41, 42, 60, 66, 67, *72*
MGM Records 67, 111, 137, 179-180, 184, 185, 188, *Back Cover*
Micheaux, Oscar 20
"Mickey Mouse" 124-*125*, 190

Mickey's Christmas Carol (movie) 124
Miles, Bernard 187
Military Cross (medal) 80
Miller, Henry 142, 188
Miller, Mitch *120*, 185
Mills, Charles Howard 16-(*17*)-18, 162, 164, 165, 166, 168
Mills, John 87, 180
Mills, Mrs. Charles Howard (C. H.) 166
Milm, Ella 182
Milwaukee Journal 170
Mind's Eye Classics 190
"Minnie Mouse" 125, *125*, 191
Minter, Andy 198
Miracle on 34th Street (1947 movie) 85
Misner, Ernest R. (Misner School of Spoken Word) 164
Miss Hattie 99
Mister Lincoln (Broadway play) 129
Mitchell Boys' Choir 180
Mitchell, John 187
Mitchell, Norman 131, 187
Mitchell, Shirley 181, 182
Moby Dick (book) 126
Modern Audio Drama 139, 140
Mohr, Gerald 182
Monahan, Jim 192
Monitor 137, 188
Monterey Media 195
Monticello Players 169
Moorehead, Agnes *58*, 59, 79, 118, 147, 178, 179
Moran, Jackie 41, 173
Morgan, Frank 174
Mori, Yoko 196
Morrera, Tom 192

Morrison, Brett 119, 133, 183
Mount, Tom 195
Mouseketeers 85
Mr. Magoo's Christmas Carol (TV special) 15, *123*-124, 149
"Mr. Magoo" 15, *123*, 149, 189
Mr. Pickwick's Christmas (record) 103, 118
Muenz, Richard 197
Muller, Stephen *104*, 176
Mulligan, Hugh 131, 186
Muni, Scott 147, 192
Munier, Ferdinand *104*, 176
Murphy, Paul W. 184
Murray, Lyn (Lynn) 181, 187
Museum of Broadcast Communications 144, 193
Mutel (music) Library 186
Mutual Broadcasting System (MBS) 67-70, 76, 79-*80*, 175, 176, 179, 181, 182, 185
Myers, Joanna 194
Nadel, William 18, 26, 49, 104, 137, 140-141, 146-147, 174, 181, 200
Napier, Alan 132
Nash Motor Company 33, 173
Nash, Clarence 125, 191
National Broadcasting Company (NBC) 18, 25-*27*, *40*, 55, *56*, *80*, 168, 171, 181, 184, 188, 199
National Players 169
National Public Radio (NPR) 140, 194
Nativity Story 43, 162
Naxos Audiobooks 197
NBC Thesaurus Syndication 26, 41, 173, 181, 199

Nebel, Long John (John Zimmerman) 145-147, 189
Neer, Dan 192
Neer, Richard 192
Neese, Tim 198
Nesbitt, John *67*, 180
Neumann, Christine 196
New York American 34, 173
New York City Opera 99
New York Evening Post 32-33
New York Herald Tribune 34, 173
New York Times 77, 168-173, 178
New York University (NYU) 149
Newman, Fred 199
News Of The Religious World (newspaper column) 162
Nichols, Ghislaine 154, 194
Nichols, Ora 174, 198
Nienhuis, Terry 198
Nigel Brooks Singers 192
Night Kitchen Radio Theater 156, 197
Nolan, David 154, 194
Nolan, Lloyd 200
Normand, Jacques 180
Norris, Randy 196
Norwood Singers 190
Nostalgia Digest 33
Novello, Jay 108
Nugent, Helen 170
Nyland, Andy 197
O'Herlihy, Dan *127*-129, 139, 186
O'Reilly, Brendan 199
Oboler, Arch 107-108, 110
O'Brien, Shannon 197
Ogg, Sammy 182
Ohio State Players 170
Old Baptist Church (Manahawkin, NJ) 155, *155*, 197

Olean (NY) Times 169
Oliver, Shirling 176
Olivier, Laurence 88, 89, 121, 138, 184
Olsen, George 32, 173
Olson, Diana 192
Omnivox Records 200
On Borrowed Time (Broadway play) 98
On Borrowed Time (radio play) 73
On The Air Today (newspaper column) 32
One Man's Family 109
Oregonian (Portland, OR) 16-18
Ork, Rick Roberts 184
Orr, Corinne 132-133, 189
Orson Welles Archive (Collection) 156
Osborne, Ted 174, 181
Oscar (Academy Award) 32, 85, 118, 159
O'Shea, Milo 131, 186
Ossman, David 142, 188
Owen, Bill 78, 147
Owen, Reginald 42, 88, 174, 183
Owen, Tudor 182
Owens, Ronn 191
Pace, Garrett 198
Pacey, Steven 192
Pacific Pioneer Broadcasters 111
Pacifica Stations 200
Paley Center for Media, NY (former Museum of Television and Radio) 155, 199, 200
Paley, William 18,
Palmer, Geoffrey 129, 194
Palumbo, Leslie 196
Pape, Cynthia 197

Paperback Audio 191
Pappas, Nikos 196
Parish, Prof. Wayland M. 164, 165, 168, 169
Parker, Elizabeth 193
Parrotti, Laura 196
Parsons, Louella 173
Paskman, Dailey 111-(*112*)-113, 137, 179
Patmore, Derek 184
Peach, Denise 192
Pearl Harbor 103
Pearson, Gigi 183
Peary, Hal 75
Penguin Audiobooks 194
Pennick & Ford, Ltd 185
"Penny Pitch" charity drive 145
Pernin, Rev. C. J. 165
Perrin, Vic (Victor) 119, 182, 183
Peter Absolute 44, 47
Peter Pan (1953 film) 74
Peter Pan Records *122*, 189
Peters, Ken 179
Peters, Margot 39-40
Pettingell, Frank 126, 186
Pfleeger, George 100
Phelps, Buster 34, 173
Phil Harris/Alice Faye Show 73
Philadelphia Record (newspaper) 39
Philco (radio/tv manufacturer) 65, 184
Phipps, William 182
Photoplay Award 109
Pickles, Vivian 138, 194
Pickwick Papers, The 10, 103, 118
Pirodsky, Richard 149
Play Night 16, 164
Playmakers 168

Playten, Alice 197
Polydor Records 133, 189
Polygram 180
Poney, Brian 182
Portraits From Dickens (record) 189
Powell, Dick 173
Power, Henry 194
Powers, Mala 181
Prave, John *153*, 154, 194
Preston, Walter 176
Proffitt, Amanda 198
Public Radio Exchange (PRX) 140, 155
Pug, Algy 198
Pyatt, Keith 182
Pyne, Joe 146
Quicksilver Radio Theater 149-(*153, 155*)-156, 158, 159, 194, 196-197
Quiet, Please 96
"R.W." (reviewer) 126, 132, 186
Radio Broadcasting News (newpaper column) 166
Radio *Carol* Stock Company 55, 69, 79, 90, 140
Radio Once More (webcast) 146
Radio Scrapbook (WJTN) *101*
Rains, Claude 121, 187
Range, Charles 176
Rashada 198
Rathbone, Basil 34, 78-79, 80-(*82*-83, 85, 105-*107*,109-110, 117, 121, 126, 140-*141*, 177-179, 185-187, 189
Rathbone, Cynthia 81, 178
Rattazzi, Steven 197
Rayburn, Gene 137, 188

RCA Victor Records 18, *93*, 95, 100, 119, 162, 176, 182, 184, 200
Readick, Frank 53, 174, 175
Reagan, Fay 107
Red Network (NBC) *80*, 168
Red Ryder 108
Reddington, Linda 197
Redfield Arts 195
Redfield, Mark 129, 195
Redfield, William 139, 191
Regency Players 189
Reitz, William H. 162
Rejman, April 197
Renkin, Dan 155, 196
Reuben's Restaurant 44
Rhodehamel, Carl 166
Rice, Frederick 197
Richards, Susan 182
Richardson, David 198
Richardson, Ralph 88, 131, 132, 138, 187, 188
Richmond (VA) Newsleader 175
Riddle, Randy A. *83*
Riley, James Whitcomb 165
Rip Van Winkle (Lionel Barrymore record) 116
Ripp, Elizabeth 191
Road to Mandalay, The (radio poem) 168
Robbins, Jerry 197
Roberts, Chris 145, 193
Robertson, Stuart 177
Robinson, Ed 176
Robinson, Jalen 199
Robinson, Larry 98, 176
Roche, Dominick 131, 186
Rockwell, Norman 34
Roediger, Rebekah 196

Roediger, Thaddaeus 196
Rogers, Michael 154
Rogers, Tawna 196
Rogers, William 149
Rohrig, Dan 198
Roosevelt, Franklin 68
Roscoe, Joseph 177
Rose, Ralph 182
Rosen, Gary 192
Ross, David 170, 171
Roth, Guy 180
Rougicek, George 187
Roy Dotrice 129, *130*, 138, 140, 191, 192
Roy, Lise 180
Royal National Institute of Blind People ("Talking Books") 139
Ruddock, John 138, 188
Rudolph the Red-Nosed Reindeer (TV special) 133
Rudy Vallee Show, The (see also Sealtest Show, Vallee Varieties) 41, 55, *56, 80,* 176, 177
Russell, Dave 192
Rutgers University Glee Club 138, 184, 187
Rutherford, Ann 42, 174
Saab 198
Sackler, Howard 187
Sag Harbor (Long Island) Express 199
Sagan, Robin 192
Salerno, Christina 196
Saltimieras, Paul 177
Salvation Army, The 86
Sands, Myra 195
Sandusky (OH) Register 170
Sanford, Erskine 53, 175

"Santa Claus (Kris Kringle)" *56*, 66, 71, 79, 85, 99, 189, 200
Santos, Gil 195
Saturday Evening Post, The (magazine) 34, 173
Saxon, Steve 190
Scarlett Rat Entertainment 197
Scelsa, Vin 147, 192
Schaefer, John 199
Schangagel, Harold 184
Scheinman, Tony 154, 194
Schiller, Danny 194
Schirmer, Bruce 191
Schmid, Max 149
Schneider, Jay 142, 191
Schreiner, Bess Davis 184
Schumann-Heink, Madame Ernestine *27,* 32, 173
Scofield, Paul 131, 132, 187, 193
Scott, George C. 59, 139
Scrapbook 19
Scrooge (1970 movie musical) 88, 142, 190
Scrooge (aka *A Christmas Carol*) (1951 movie) 140
Scrooge (Part 1 – Marley's Ghost; Part 2 – The Ghost of Christmas Past) (record) 162
Scrooge (stage musical) 111
"Scrooge McDuck" 124-*125*, 190
Scrooge, or, Marley's Ghost (movie) 12
Scrooge, the Miser's Dream (stage play) 11
Scrooge's Awakening (1905 record) 13, 162
Scrooge's Christmas Morning (aka *Scrooge's Awakening*) (1905/1906 record) 13, 162

Sealtest Show, The (see also The Rudy Vallee Show) 55, *80*, 176, 177
Searle, Ronald 149
Sears Radio Theater 108
Seattle Daily Times 164, 166
Seebach, Julius 170
Seldes, Marian 139, 191
Seymour, Dan *48*
"Shadow, The (Lamont Cranston)" 119, 133
Shakespeare, William ("The Bard") 19, 51, 65, 80, 118, 133
Shallenberg, Kara 198
Shanks, Rosilind 188
Sharp, Tim 196
Shaw, George Bernard 79
Shepherd's Hey, The (music) 49
Sherlock Holmes (radio play) 44
Sherlock Holmes (radio series) 26, 98, 104, 132, 171
"Sherlock Holmes" 26, 44, 53, 78, 80, 98, 104, 131, 132, 171
Sherlock, Philip 195
Sherman, Hiram 46, 174
Shinn, Everett 61
Shirley, Alfred 45, 47, 98, 174, 176
Shope, Henry 176
Showboat (radio series) 25
Shutta, Ethel 32, 173
Sievers, Bob 145, 193
Sill, Kerry 196
Sill, Nick 196
Silver, Jeffrey 181, 182
Sim, Alistair 140
Simmons, Jean 88, 180
Simon & Schuster Audio *134*, 135, 194
Simone, Mark 146-147, 193

Sinclair, Ronald 174
Singer, Simon "Stuffy" 63, 70, 98, 183
Singing Story Lady, The (also see Wicker, Ireene) 199
Sirius/XM 156, 197
Sirius/XM Radio 156, 197
Sirott, Bob 193
Siskind, Ronald K. 188
Skimos, Jim 145, 192, 193
Sloane, Everett 53, 90, 175, 179
Small One, The (radio) 66
Small One, The (record) 103
Smith, Bob 119, 185, 197
Smith, Bob 197
Smith, "Buffalo Bob" 119-*120*, 185
Smith, Edward H. 163
Smith, Kate 66
Smith, Terrence J. 196
Sneed, Michael 193
Snowden, Eric 55, 69, *104*, 175, 177, 181-183
Soanes, Jack *21*, 24, 170, 171
Soconyland Sketches 25, 26, 170, 171
Son of Frankenstein (movie) 80
Sorrell, Jeanne 188
Soule, Olan 175
Soundelux cassettes 189
Soundhouse Ltd. 195
South Boston 94
Spann, Owen 191
Speaight, Frank 172
Speed Racer (TV series) 132
"Speedy Alka-Seltzer" 76
SPERDVAC (Society to Preserve and Encourage Radio Drama, Variety and Comedy) 110
Spider-Man (1967 TV series) 133

Spingold, Harry W. 169, 170
Spoken Arts Records 186
Spoken Word America 156, 197
Spoken Word Dickens (record) 190
Spoken Words (radio) 200
Springfield (MA) Republican 16, 163, 166, 167
Spurgeon, Jeff 199
St. Charles Players 195
Children's Bookwatch (publication) 195
 St. Chrysostom's Choir (Chicago) 170
St. Clair, Leonard 76, 183
St. Edmunds Episcopal Church (Chicago) 162
Stafford Township Historical Society 155, *155*, 197
Stafford, Anna, 48, 174
Stafford, Hanley 174
Staley, Dr. Delbert M. 166
Star Trek: The Next Generation (TV series) 133
Star Wars (movie) 88
Starky, Joe 191
Stars Over Hollywood 80,*80*, 81, *82*, 85-87, 178, 181-183
Statzer, Bob 142
Steigerwald, John 198
Stella Dallas 119
Stephenson, John 76, 183
Sterling Milk Co. *143*, 188
Sterling Productions 190
Sterling Records 13-*14*, 162
Stern, Jay 150-(*153*)-155, 194
Stevens, Carl 195
Stevens, Francis *60*
Stevens, Leith 80, 105, 177

Stevens, Sydney 200
Stewart, James 110
Stewart, Patrick 133-(*134*)-135, 194
Stingiest Man in Town, The (TV, stage, radio, CD) 140-*141*, 189
Stone, Anne 177
Story Time 138, 189, 190
Stow, Rupert 199
Strack, Amy 197
Streamlined Shakespeare 39, *40*
Street, Jessica 196
Studebaker, Hugh 175
Studio 1 (One) (CBS radio) 44, *45*, *48*, 50
Stull, Elizabeth 154, 194
Stump, Liberty 198
Stutter, Mervyn 195
Suchet, David 140, 195
Sutton, Art 184
Sutton, Brad 170
Sweeney, Bob *67*, 74, 180
Swift, Allen 119, 185
Syms, Joe Richard 195
Syms, Sylvia 181
Syracuse (NY) Herald 166
Syracuse University 166
Taliaferro, Ray 191
Talking Book, A *127*, 129, 186
Tarkington, Booth 43
Taylor, Burk C. 165
Taylor, Deems 188
Terris, Tom 162, 172
Tetley, Walter 105, 109, 177
Thackeray, William Makepeace 15
Thatcher, Heather 104, 176
Thayer, Tom 193
Theatre Royal 89, 184
Thomason, James 192

Thompson, Duane *104*, 176
Thompson, Josh 198
Thompson, Mike 193
Thorson, Cliff 175
Thorton, Frank 200
Thousand Oaks Library 87
Throckmorton, Levi 198
Timberg, Sammy 179
Times, The (Henderson, NC newspaper) 116
Today on the Radio (newspaper column) 171, 172
Today's Radio Program (newspaper column) 162-167
Toledo (OH) Blade 188
Tomczak, Mike 193
Tony Award 139, 154
Too Many Cooks 74
Top Rank (Vanguard) Records 131, 186
Torch, Sidney 184
Toscanini, Arturo 18
Tots 'N' Teens (Regal) Records 116, *117*, 180
Towers of London (prod. co.) 180
Towers, Harry Alan 87, 89, 132, 184
Treacher, Arthur 132
Treasure Island (radio play) 44, *48*, 72
Treasury Star Parade ("A Modern Scrooge") 57, 177
Trenton (NJ) Times 163,165
Treves, Fredrick 138
Trevor, Bob 192
Triangle Players 165
Troop, Prof. J. G. C. 167
Trot, Arlene 191
Truman, Ralph 138, 188

Turner Network Television (TNT) 133
Turner, J.T. 197
Turner, James 197
Tuscaloosa News 111, 185
Tuttle, Lurene 84, 105, 177, 181
'Twas the Night Before Christmas (record poem) 189
Twelfth Night (radio play) 39
Tyson, Julia 199
U.S. (United States) Steel 132
Ugly Duckling, The (radio story) 199
Uncle Don Carney (Howard Rice) 98
Underwood, Jack 145, 192
Underwood, Jeffrey 182
United Press (UP) 18
United Transcription Service 199
University of Cincinnati 163
University of Florida 129
University of Pittsburgh 164, 168, 169
Updike, Diana 193
Vallee Varieties (see also The Rudy Vallee Show) *56*, 177
Vallee, Rudy 41, 55, *56, 80*, 176, 177
Van Patten, Dick (Dickie, Richard) 25, 98, 99
Van Wye, Prof. 163
Vanguard (Top Rank) Records 131, 186
Variety (newspaper) 32, 54, 69, 70, 90, 117, 175, 184
Vaughan, Tristan 199
Victor Records (see RCA VICTOR)
Visit from St. Nicholas, A (radio poem) 167
Vivian, Robert 26, *27*, 171

Index

W2XE New York 20-23, 170
WABC New York 20, 21-23, 28, 34, 81-*82*,170-172, 179, 185, 188
WADC Akron *21*,169
Wade, Philip 173
WAIT Chicago 180
WAIU Columbus, OH 171
Waldo, Janet 125, 191
Wallace, Gordon 184
Walsh, Ronnie 186
Walz, Jay 97, 176
WAMU Wash., D.C. 159
Washington (D.C.) Post 32, 38, 39, 97, 164, 172, 173, 176, 179
Washington Chapel Players 184
Waterman, Willard 175
Watkins, Linda 196
Watkinson, Eve 186
Waxman, Franz 174
WBAI New York 149, *153*, 154, 187, 194
WBAL Baltimore 200
WBBM Chicago *67*
WBET Boston 168
WBZ Springfield (later Boston) MA 145, 166, 195
WCAP Wash., D.C. 164
WCFM Wash., D.C. 90, 184
WEAF New York 16, *17*, 18, *80*, 90, 142, 162-166, 168, 170, 171
WEAO Columbus 170
Weatherford, Russ – *Back Cover*
Webcast 156, 197
Wechsler, Maria 197
WEEI Boston166
Weems, Harriette 166, 168
Weiss, Jim 130, 195
Weldon, Martin 182

Welles, Orson 18, *31*, 41-(*45, 48*)-55, 89, 110, 111, 119, 132, 135, 149, 156, 174, 175, 183, 198
Wells, George 103, *104*, 175
Wells, H.G. (Herbert George) 132
Wessel, William 164, 166
Western Carolina University 50, 156, *157, 158*
Westfield (NJ) Leader 184
Westminster Records 186
WFBH New York 165, 166
WFBL Syracuse 18, 166, 168
WGBH Boston 159
WGBS New York 165, 172
WGES Chicago 90, 177
WGN Chicago 19, *66, 71*, 165, 167, 168, 169, 170, 171, 175
WGY Schenectady 16, 18, 163, 166
WHBI Newark 191
Whealey, David 196
Whelan, Albert 13-*14*, 95, 162
Whelen, Christopher 188
Whitaker, Janet 193
White Christmas (Irving Berlin music)
White House, The 68
White, Lew 176
White, Matthew 195
Whiteside, Adele 184
Whitfield, Anne 74, 183
WHK Cleveland 164, 169
WHN New York 43
WICC Bridgeport, CT 168
Wichman, Craig 150, *153, 155*, 174, 181, 194, 196, *Back Cover*
Wick, Bob 155, 196
Wicker, Ireene ("The Singing Lady") 116, 117, 118, 180, 188, 199
Wilcox, Harlow 58, 105, 109, 177

Wilde, Colette 187
Willcocks, David 187
William and Mary (College) Players 175
Williams, Bransby 13-*14*, 95, 126,162, 186
Williams, Emlyn 200
Williams, Ewen 192
Williams, Rhoda 108, 177
Wilmer, Douglas 131, 187
Wilson, Dick (Richard) 46, *48*
Wilson, J. Donald 178
Wilson, Jo Manning 188
Wilson, Meredith 174
Wimbush, Mary 188
Wimbush, Roger 190
WIND Chicago 80, 177
Wing, Anna 194
Winkler, Bobby *107*
Winnipeg Free Press 163, 165
Winocur, Mary 188
WINS 185
Winslowe, Paula 108, 177
Winters, Jonathan 140, 159, 194
Wired For Books (online site) 135, 196
Wisconsin State Journal 54, 55, 175, 179, 188
"Witch (from Snow White") (Disney character) *125*
Withers, Googie 88, 180
Witwer, Kathryn 173
WJMA Orange, VA 137, 188
WJR Pontiac, MI 170
WJTN Jamestown, NY 100, *102*, 176
WJZ New York 166, 169, 171, 172
WKRC Cincinnati 169

WLAG Minneapolis 163
WLIB Elgin, IL 165, 166
WLS Chicago 19, 164, 167, 169
WLUP-AM Chicago 143-145, 193
WLW Cincinatti 163, 165
WLWL New York 172
WMAK Lockport, NY. 18, 166
WMAL Wash., D.C. 169
WMAQ Chicago 16, *56*, 164
WMC Memphis 163
WMCA New York 146, 193
WMES Boston 167
WMMG Brandenburg, KY 142, 191
WMXF Waynesville, NC 197
WNBC New York 145, 189
WNEW-FM New York 147, 192
WNYC New York 159, 165-168, 188, 199, 200
WOAW Omaha 16, 164
WOL Wash., D.C. 90, 179
Wolf, Bruce 193
Wonderland Records (see also A.A., Golden) 122, 123, 188, 189, 192
Wong, Barbara Jean 55, 103, *104*, 175, 177
Wong, Tony 191
Wons, Tony (Anthony Snow) 19, 169
WONW Defiance, OH 103
Woods, Leslie 98, 99, 176
Woodthorpe, Peter 194
Woollcott, Alexander 29, 32, 172, 173
WOR New York /Newark 16, 18, 79-*80*, 90, 146, 162, 164, 167-170, 172, 176, 179, 185
Works Progress Administration (WPA) 46

World War I 80, 121
World War II 67
World Wide Web 156, 197
Worth, Frank 182
WOUB (Ohio University) Center for Public Media 196
WOWO Ft. Wayne 145, 192
WPPB Southampton, NY 159, 199
WQXR New York 159, 182, 199
WRC Wash., D.C. 16, 163, 178
WRDC Hartford 171
Wreford, Edgar 187
Wright, Ben 179, 182
Wrigley's (Co.) *67*
WRNC Ashland, WI 159
WRNL Richmond 90, 175
WRNY New York 168, 169
WSPD Toledo 169
WTOD-AM & FM Toledo, OH 142, *143*, 188

Wuthering Heights (1939 movie) 89
WVNJ Newark, NJ 137, 184, 187
WWDC Wash., D.C. 180
WWL New Orleans 159
WWNC Ashville, NC 174, 197
Wyatt, Eustace 49, 97, 98, 100, 174, 176
Wyncote, Andrew 194
Wynn, Ed 63
WYRS Manahawkin, NJ 155, *155*, 196
Yorinks, Arthur 197, 199
Young, Alan 124-125, 190, 191
Young, David 176
Young, Loretta 103
Young, Robert 42, 174
Young, Victor 32, *104*, 173, 175
Zamparelli, Joseph 197
Ziv (radio production co.) *83*
Zumhagen, Brian 199

Author's Bio

Craig Wichman is an actor, writer, producer, and lifelong lover of Charles Dickens' *A Christmas Carol*.

He is also the founder of the modern audio drama group Quicksilver Radio Theater, with whom he has played such legendary characters as Frankenstein's Monster and Ebenezer Scrooge, and which has taken awards from the National Federation of Community Broadcasters and the National Audio Theatre. And he was a longtime performer at the Friends of Old Time Radio conventions, where his roles in recreations of vintage scripts ranged from Sherlock Holmes to Shakespeare's Cassius, and where he was honored to join the ranks of several veteran radio actors as a recipient of the Florence Williams Award.

Craig is the creator of the short film *A Christmas Carol–In Eight Minutes*, was nominated for a Best Actor Award at the Chicago Horror Film Festival for his work in the title role of *The Devil You Know*, created a role in the premiere of the acclaimed Off-Broadway show *The Bardy Bunch*, and will soon be seen in the feature film *The Adventures Of Paul And Marian*.

As a writer his work includes scripts for Quicksilver and Openhousenewyork, articles about the *Carol* in *Nostalgia Digest* and *Radio Recall*, about Christ as a character in motion pictures in *The Lutheran*, and about his personal impressions of the 9/11 attack for his hometown newspaper, Defiance, Ohio's *Crescent-News*.

Craig lives in New York City with his classical singer wife Bernadette and their orange tabby Tyler.

Corrections and additions to the information contained in this book are welcomed by the author, especially for those productions for which some facts are still uncertain. Information about where to obtain recordings of many of the broadcasts discussed in these pages can also be obtained at the same email address, QuicksilverRT@aol.com.

CHRISTMAS PAST IS GONE... CHRISTMAS FUTURE IS NOT YET HERE... BUT *A CHRISTMAS CAROL* IS EVER PRESENT.

www.ingramcontent.com/pod-product-compliance
Lightning Source LLC
Chambersburg PA
CBHW071434150426
43191CB00008B/1125